saving the world at work

saving the world at work

WHAT COMPANIES AND INDIVIDUALS CAN DO TO GO BEYOND MAKING A PROFIT TO MAKING A DIFFERENCE

TIM SANDERS

DOUBLEDAY

NEW YORK   LONDON   TORONTO   SYDNEY   AUCKLAND

ꓒꓒ

DOUBLEDAY

Published in the United States by Doubleday, an imprint of The Doubleday
Publishing Group, a division of Random House, Inc., New York.
www.doubleday.com

DOUBLEDAY is a registered trademark and the DD colophon is a trademark of
Random House, Inc.

Book design by Tina Henderson

Library of Congress Cataloging-in-Publication Data
Sanders, Tim.
Saving the world at work : what companies and individuals can do to go
beyond making a profit to making a difference / by Tim Sanders.—1st ed.
p. cm.
Includes index.
1. Social responsibility of business—Handbooks, manuals, etc. I. Title.
HD60.S247 2008
658.4'08—dc22
2008018401

ISBN 978-0-385-52357-8

PRINTED IN THE UNITED STATES OF AMERICA

1 3 5 7 9 10 8 6 4 2

First Edition

To Jacqueline, who saved my world

Contents

PART I The Responsibility Revolution   1

  1 The Power of One Revolutionary   3

  2 The Nature of Business Revolutions   16

  3 Phase One: A Change in Circumstances   25

  4 Phase Two: The Rise of a New Value System   30

  5 Phase Three: The Arrival of the Innovators   44

  6 Phase Four: Disruption   68

  7 Phase Five: The New Order   86

PART II The Saver Soldier   93

  8 The Six Laws of the Saver Soldier   95

PART III The Practice of Being Good   117

  9 Assess   119

  10 Act: Save Your People   125

  11 Act: Save Your Communities   159

  12 Act: Save Your Planet   177

  13 Influence   204

  14 Good Gravy: The Power of Being a Saver Soldier   222

  15 If Not You, Then Who?   226

Acknowledgments   235

Index   237

PART I

The Responsibility Revolution

1

The Power of One Revolutionary

There is a revolution under way, one that will change the way people define the role of business.

There is a revolution under way that will undermine billion-dollar companies if they don't respond to it, and make niche companies that embrace it enormously valuable.

There is a revolution under way that will transform our reasons for buying products and services. This revolution will be more influential than the quality revolution of the 1970s or the Internet revolution of the 1990s.

There is a revolution under way that will rival compensation and benefits as the primary reason to take a job.

If you're not paying attention to this revolution, you and your company may be running out of time to participate—and thrive in the post-revolutionary era.

The Responsibility Revolution has arrived. It demands that companies make a difference to society—not just indirectly, by producing jobs and profits, but directly, through their products, through their manufacturing methods and operational systems, through their environmental efforts and community outreach.

The consumers and customers leading this revolution will screen your company to see if it is socially responsible. Then, and only then, will they reward it with their loyalty.

The Responsibility Revolution represents a new consciousness among consumers concerning why we buy or don't buy, what we use or don't use. We want to make a positive difference with our wallets, and through our actions, to make the world a better place.

There is also a new consciousness among employees. We want to find greater meaning in our lives through our work. We want to be associated with companies that practice good corporate citizenship.

There is a new consciousness among investors as well. We want to shape the future by putting our money into companies that match our social values.

Consumers, employees, and investors are changing business. They expect the companies with which they do business to join them in taking responsibility for the planet on which we all live, and for giving back to the larger world.

This is not a revolution that can be ignored. It will not go away. If your business isn't socially responsible in the future, the forces of good will ride into the market like the cavalry, surround it, and choke off your supply lines. If you work in a company that is not socially responsible, whether it is a Fortune 500 company or a mom-and-pop operation, it will feel the impact on its profits and revenues, and your colleagues could lose their jobs as the company buckles under the weight of this new paradigm.

You don't believe me? Consider this: Today 65 percent of Americans are willing to switch to a brand associated with a good cause if price and quality are relatively equal. And 66 percent participate in at least one social cause-generated boycott each year (and with each passing year, the percentage grows).

In a recent study by the global consultancy The Work Foundation,

10 percent of young job seekers identified themselves as "ethical enthusiasts," more concerned about the ecological values of their potential employer than they are about starting take-home pay. One-third of these job seekers will be looking for a new position soon, because they feel their employers' contribution to the community is below par. Two-thirds of this year's college graduates claim they will not work for a company with a poor reputation for social responsibility.

Even more like-minded individuals will hit the workforce in 2010. In a 2006 study of fourteen- to eighteen-year-olds (commissioned by ad agency Energy BBDO), 78 percent said money "was less important to them than personal fulfillment." They went on to work for "companies that promote equality, a green environment, and social responsibility." For them, purpose trumps paycheck.

Need more evidence? Socially responsible investments (SRIs)—mutual funds that screen companies for their contributions to society—rose 258 percent in the last ten years, a return on investment that beats the market by more than 15 percent. SRIs have grown in volume from $235 billion in 1995 to $2.3 trillion in 2005, which is twice the amount of money that came together a decade ago to fund the dotcom revolution. Financial analysts are starting to factor in the long-term risks of a company that pollutes, treats its workers poorly, or ignores the communities in which it operates—even if these companies are swimming in profits today.

Do you want to be part of a great company? If so, you need to understand that "great" is getting an extreme makeover. Today, *good* is the new great.

A good company is one whose mission is to improve the lives of everyone in its footprint: employees, suppliers, customers, supporting communities, and the planet.

Customers, workers, and investors are flipping the basic charter for business on its head. Making money, producing profits, paying taxes, and providing employment opportunity are not enough. Companies now must directly improve the world around them. Adding value to employees, the community, and the planet will be critical in the twenty-first century.

A landmark study by business consultants McKinsey & Company, *The War for Talent*, claims that the recruitment and retention of talent in management and leadership positions will be the key to maintaining a competitive advantage in the future.

Businesses are chasing too few dollars with too many products, according to research from industries as diverse as retail and high technology; there is a war raging for customers and their loyalty. This war will determine which companies will prosper in the future and which companies will be running on fumes.

As Wall Street recognizes, market valuation and the ability to raise investment capital are the keys to expansion. The battle for investment dollars is fierce. Without the oxygen of fresh capital and loyal investors, new companies cannot grow and mature companies cannot compete.

So who is behind the Responsibility Revolution?

I call the people who compose its growing chorus the Them Generation. Many of them were born after 1980, but its membership includes everybody, of any age, who is focused on "them"—that is, on others.

Growing up in the 1960s, I was part of the Me Generation. We were only one generation removed from the Great Depression. I lived a life of material scarcity: I thought primarily about me, my safety, my security, and my future. Some called it self-involvement; I thought of it as survival.

The Me Generation was superseded in the 1980s and 1990s by the Us Generation, a group that focused half on me, half on you. This is basically the same story, same theme. What's in it for me? What's in it for us?

By comparison, the Them Generation sees itself as affluent rather than impoverished. These people don't expect merely to survive, but to thrive. To them, there is enough to go around, and they are making a cause of giving some of it to others. They have little connection to the fear and insecurity of the Great Depression. Even speed bumps in the economy, such as the mortgage industry meltdown of 2007, don't faze this group—they believe that these market lows will be followed by new market highs in the near future. They aren't obsessed with notions of scarcity, survival, and security. They've moved up Abraham Maslow's psychological ladder to a higher emotional need: to achieve significance.

Over half of all college students volunteered for a community or social project in 2007, up 50 percent from a previous generation; they are quickly becoming part of a purpose-driven economy, one that searches for meaning in work, career, and business. These students are focused on the faceless millions who have no voice, the impoverished workers in South America and underage children in Asia making our products. Them. The outside world.

Because the Them Generation wants to make the world a better place, they expect business to help. To achieve these goals, "Them-Geners" have become economic activists. They are a "smart mob" (a term invented by futurist Howard Rheingold), people who have the capacity to coordinate and collaborate with other people electronically to elicit change. They are wired to the gills and smart with their tools, proficient at text and instant messaging, blogging, e-mailing, social networking, and working the World Wide Web. They can make things happen, overnight.

Consumers today are able to find out anything, anytime, anywhere, aided by gossip Web sites, YouTube, and a host of other emerging digital tattletales. Little stays secret in today's society. Your company's actions and intentions will be revealed and posted somewhere on a blog or a bulletin board for all to read and forward.

As the century marches on, your social intentions will be more important to success than your business concept. A recent survey indicates that almost half of all consumers use the Internet to figure out if the actions we take and the products we buy are socially responsible. These are thumb warriors, with a cause.

Finally, ThemGeners are highly influential. Much as Microsoft chairman Bill Gates swayed investor Warren Buffett to give away most of his money to others, today's young revolutionaries are recruiting their elders to the cause. These fresh recruits—our parents and grandparents—have time to spare and fat retirement accounts. They represent one of the fastest-growing segments of new Internet users. They start out sending e-mail pictures of their grandkids and wind up sending mass e-mails of petitions, telling their friends to stop shopping at Wal-Mart or to boycott Exxon.

Washington, too, is contributing to the revolution in fits and starts. Reeling from corporate scandals, from WorldCom to Enron, the government has passed new legislation with teeth, compelling companies to comply or die. Legislation such as the 2002 Sarbanes-Oxley bill requires total transparency on the part of businesses in accounting and reporting. It creates a platform for government lawsuits against businesses with questionable ethical practices. It punishes repeat offenders with escalating fines. It penalizes socially irresponsible businesses by locking them out of billions of dollars of government contract work.

Government is even beginning to penalize socially inefficient companies. The Oregon State legislature is considering a punitive tax on printing paper that would effectively double its price. Several other states are looking at similar taxes on a wide range of forest products, including wood and paper. Three separate, bipartisan bills in Congress seek to tax a company's carbon emissions beyond a set limit.

Companies that focus solely on profits are out of sync with the times. It's not enough to have your mission statement read: Make the shareholders rich. Such "shareism," or worshiping at the church of the stock price, is no longer enough.

Protecting the share price is constantly trotted out as an excuse for a company to refrain from doing the right thing for its customers, its employees, and society. And it keeps almost everyone at the company from thinking outside of a ninety-day box.

Under the impetus of shareism, a company can easily become shortsighted and inward-looking. Shareism sucks the energy and spirit out of companies, trapping them in a vicious cycle, seeing only this year's profit-and-loss statement and, in doing so, ultimately driving away customers, employees, and the larger community.

The fact is, customers don't care about the price of the company's stock or the financial return to its shareholders. But they do care about shortsighted programs that fly in the face of their values and pollute their world.

When shareism dominates a company, its team's energy is whipsawed by the floating price of the stock and the health of the profit-sharing plan. If the stock is down because of an analyst's negative report, so is employee attendance that day. More people call in sick.

Those who do come to work have that deer-in-the-headlines look on their faces and have a hard time concentrating on work.

When leaders at an airline decide to cut the flight attendants' pension plan to put a penny back in the earnings-per-share pool, not surprisingly passengers encounter surly attendants the next day.

When the stock is a company's only yardstick, it thinks less about the future and circles the wagons. Quality, innovation, service excellence, and profits dry up. If you're IBM, DEC, or GM, and profits are your only end game, my attitude is ABCya—wouldn't want to be ya.

Companies that are in business for good are already beginning to take your company's market share. These are the pioneers of the Responsibility Revolution. Everyone wants to work for them. Customers increasingly stand in line to buy from them. And investors are beginning to seek them out.

Can you see the dark storm clouds forming? Do you hear the rising thunder? To companies stuck in the profit-is-everything mode, those are the approaching signs of companies such as Whole Foods that have embraced the idea that profit is a means to change the world—in Whole Foods' case, to make the world a healthier place.

Other pioneers, such as SAS Institute (technology), Medtronic (medical care), Lush (retail), Timberland (manufacturing), and Interface (carpeting), are helping to set the pace, running ahead of the pack. They suffer some setbacks as they blaze the trail into unknown business territories, but I guarantee you they have few regrets.

Their stock's price-to-earnings ratio is higher than that of their less socially focused competitors; they are outperforming their rivals when measured against everything from profit to talent retention. They are satisfying their customers while letting them feel good about their patronage, and they're scaring the heck out of the traditional just-for-profit companies, who are scratching their heads over whether this is a fad or the new paradigm.

The premise of *Saving the World at Work* is simple. I want to recruit you, and train you, for the Responsibility Revolution. I want to help you feel good about your company and grow more good within it. I want to help you feel more fulfilled by your job, by helping your company to see the value of giving back to the larger world.

I believe the Responsibility Revolution will redefine innovation, branding, leadership, management excellence, and courage in the business world—because being good will not be easy. Individuals and businesses will need to develop what I call business social skills.

Among these skills: How can I properly link my personal goals with my company's business goals and add social value? How can I do it without a great deal of funding? How can I help to reduce my company's social inefficiency?

For many of you, this challenge will require developing a new type of business acumen. You may need to undo much of your on-the-job training in traditional P&L statements. You may have to learn to factor in your environmental footprint and the cost in human profits and losses. You may have to shift your thinking from narrow monthly or quarterly time frames to a much longer time horizon. You may have to learn how to design—or redesign—your business life to create a win/win for yourself, the company, *and* society. You may have to ask tough questions aloud, such as "Is this good for the company? Is this good for the world?"

You will most likely have to learn how to measure items you've never been taught to measure before: quality of life, clean air and water, the financial impact of goodwill, the financial risks of relying on nonrenewable and unsustainable materials, and the business value of improving local economic conditions.

I am speaking here to everyone from the mailroom to the board-room. No matter who you are, or where you work, or how high up or low down you are in an organization, you can make a difference. You can shape your community. You can become the catalyst to produce outreach programs that embed themselves throughout your entire company. You can change the world at work, even if you don't have a title and have never fancied yourself a leader.

Let me ask you a question: What if I told you that one person, and not the CEO, can contribute to an extreme makeover at your company? Let me give you an example:

In 1994, Joyce LaValle was a Los Angeles–based, regional sales director for Interface Inc., an office carpet maker headquartered in Atlanta. In the summer of that year, Joyce's daughter, Melissa, mailed her a copy of a book—*The Ecology of Commerce*, by environmentalist Paul Hawken.

Inside the book, Melissa had written her mother a note that read: "Mummy, you've got to get Ray Anderson [Interface's CEO] to read this book. The carpet industry is creating a big problem and you need to do something about it!"

Melissa, an environmental studies graduate of the University of Wisconsin, had heard Hawken speak at a conference and had bought the book afterward. His message convinced her that many industries, including the carpet business, were destroying the environment. He argued that the world's industrial titans were plundering the planet for profit, practicing "tyranny against future generations."

Hawken's talk, as well as his book, converted Melissa into a full-blown revolutionary, and she wanted to recruit her mother to join her. She also set her sights on CEO Ray Anderson.

At that time Ray Anderson was, he says, "at best, neutral on the subject, with a show-me-the-money attitude. Before the summer of 1994, I'd never given the environment a thought."

Starting that year, his sales team began relaying to their managers questions from clients they couldn't answer, such as "What is Interface doing to protect the environment?" Environmental consultants on the West Coast were telling sales managers that Interface "doesn't get it."

When Anderson first heard these comments, he replied, "Don't get what!?" He let the issue languish.

But back in California, Joyce read Hawken's book, became enamored with the message, and set out to find a way to get the book into Anderson's hands. Because she wasn't in a position to give it to him directly, she asked her boss at corporate headquarters, Gordon Whitener, to do so for her.

Joyce mailed Whitener the book, and Whitener casually placed it on the corner of Anderson's desk. There it sat for a few days.

What happened next, according to Anderson, was that "my research team and a few sales leaders were pressuring me to do something, and quick. They said, 'We want you to launch this task force, give it a kickoff speech, and launch it with your environmental vision.'

"I didn't have an environmental vision. And I didn't want to make that speech. But they stayed on my case, so I relented. Then I thought: What am I going to say? I couldn't think of anything except compliance, which to me was being 'as bad as the law would allow.' I knew that was not a winning vision. Then, a week before the meeting, I found this book on my desk."

He scooped it into his briefcase and, later that night, started to read it. "The book's central point was that the Earth was dying and the biggest culprit was . . . this make-waste industrial system of which my company is an integral part. I realized I was a plunderer."

Anderson slept fitfully and awoke the next day with a new business vision. He called Joyce personally, thanking her for the book. And a few days later he gave a passionate kickoff speech, explaining why this was an ethical issue that needed to be addressed immediately, and sharing his belief that he and his team were "environmental vandals, stealing from the future." By the end of the talk, almost everyone in attendance was in tears.

Anderson next put Hawken on retainer as a consultant and read dozens of other related books to expand his vision. Then he made sweeping changes throughout the company: He directed a team to slash carbon emissions in the production process (they responded by cutting them over 99 percent within four years). He commanded factories to recycle all vinyl carpet backing. His engineers redesigned carpet trimmings to dramatically reduce the amount of scraps that went into landfill. His sales team came up with a plan to lease carpet, guaranteeing that it would be properly disposed of when removed. He prohibited the use of virgin (first-use, nonrecycled), petroleum-based products.

Most significant, Anderson created a new mission statement—Mission Zero—promising to make the company environmentally neutral by the year 2020.

Within the first twelve years, Interface diverted over 100 million pounds of carpet and waste from landfills, where it would have taken tens of thousands of years to disintegrate. The waste- and energy-use-reduction programs produced the side benefit of saving the company over $300 million in the first five years.

Today, Joyce LaValle is a senior vice president and widely respected in her industry as an important contributor to Interface's environmental strategy. And Anderson continues to preach—he has now given over one thousand speeches advocating that other companies join him in climbing "Mount Sustainability." He's consulted with some of the most influential people in the business world, including his old college friend Mike Duke, the number two executive at Wal-Mart. He's challenged his biggest suppliers, such as DuPont, to step up and match his efforts. He now describes himself as a radical industrialist.

All of this came from one person's courage to follow her heart. When Anderson wrote his 1998 book *Mid-Course Correction*, he gave a special acknowledgment to Melissa LaValle, the young woman whose passion and courage helped to change the carpet industry. And when I interviewed him for the first time, looking for the seed of his own passion for sustainability, Anderson quickly cited Joyce LaValle.

That is the power of one infectious revolutionary.

2

The Nature of Business Revolutions

The word *revolution* comes from the Latin *revolutio*, which means "a turnaround." It is a complete and irreversible change that occurs in a relatively short period of time (as opposed to evolution, a great change that occurs gradually).

Revolutions are fueled by frustration with the status quo, combined with a perceived opportunity to seize the moment and alter it. Two of the most notable examples are the American and French Revolutions, but countless others—not necessarily political—follow the same pattern.

In the context of business, revolutions lead toward massive changes in the manner in which business is conducted. Harvard Business School professor Clayton Christensen, author of *The Innovator's Dilemma*, defines revolutions in business as "movements punctuated with disruptive innovations that either create new markets or reshape existing markets."

Business revolutions occur in five phases:

The first phase is a *change in circumstances* that dramatically impacts how we think about the business landscape.

Our lives are continually shaped by the social environment

in which we live. When seismic events occur, they inexorably alter the business landscape. The result is a shock to the collective consciousness that causes us to view the world in new and unexpected ways.

In some cases, the change in circumstances is beneficial, such as the dawn of the Industrial Revolution. A key driver of that revolution was a breakthrough in manufacturing technology that established the machine as a replacement for manual labor. Because they generated so much wealth and led to such dramatic savings, machines paved the way for a new mode of thinking about the production of goods.

Any major change in circumstances results in the second phase of a business revolution: *a new set of values*. In this context, my definition of values is: beliefs that shape the criteria by which one allocates resources. If you believe in corporate stability rather than strategic risk taking, your efforts will go into preserving the status quo instead of into research and development. If you value accuracy over speed, you'll invest in quality control rather than production capacity and quotas.

Businesses are always values-driven. If company leadership strives to be first in its field, it will place market share ahead of profitability as the metric of success. If a business wants to be first in technological leadership, research and development becomes the top priority.

When values shift—whether those of your company, your customers, or the country—so does the business landscape. New markets are created based on new needs and desires, and old markets shrivel up.

If customers change their minds and want something different, a company's value proposition doesn't work anymore. If no one is interested in what you have to offer, you are out of business. Giving customers and business partners what they care about is the basis for all economic competition.

A new set of values can cause a company to move from being the industry lion to the industry dinosaur.

The third phase of the business revolution is *the arrival of the innovators*. In response to new values, some perceptive companies rush in to meet the needs of underserved or emerging markets. They are the innovators, and they play the role of spoiler to the old guard. They buck the system in a way that resonates with the new values.

For example, innovative companies may offer faster instead of better or cheaper as a value proposition. Their quality may seem substandard, and their price too high, to the incumbent industry leaders. But to the new market for convenience, the innovator hits its sweet spot.

Innovators are usually early to market, entering just as the values shift, catering to early adopters at the high end of the market willing to pay a premium. They generally operate in a way that looks unattractive to the establishment, giving them time to perfect their offerings.

As the new values reach a tipping point of mass popularity, the fourth, and most extreme, phase of a business revolution occurs: *disruption*. This happens when incumbent industry leaders are either toppled or cave in to market pressures, and can only survive by making radical transformations to their business model. Earning shortfalls, layoffs, bankruptcies, and organizational overhauls litter the disruptive phase of the business revolution.

As Gary Hamel says in his book *Leading the Revolution*, "First, the revolutionaries will take your markets and your customers. Next they'll take your best employees. Finally, they'll take your assets. The barbarians are no longer banging on the gates, they are eating off your best china."

The fifth and final salvo of a business revolution is the very long period in which companies develop proficiency in serving new markets as innovators become more sophisticated and customers more demanding. I call this period *the New Order*.

Eventually, surviving companies will satisfy the new market needs and the competition will then turn to who does it best.

The Quality Revolution

A perfect example of the five-stage business revolution took place in America from the 1960s through the 1980s.

Phase One: A Change in Circumstances
During World War II, the U.S. government asked American consumers to support the war effort by doing without many goods, especially durables such as washing machines and refrigerators.

This situation changed dramatically when the war ended and millions of Americans experienced a dramatic increase in prosperity. The war machine now reverted to a consumer-goods machine, restoring production capacity, and the 1960s saw the rise of individual ownership of durable products, with a radio in every room, several televisions in every home, and two cars in every garage.

Due to their low prices, vast quantities of Asian products entered the market throughout the 1960s, especially televisions, radios, and home appliances, many of them manufactured in Japan, which had learned how to create quality appliances through a program instituted by General Douglas MacArthur and taught in part by American guru W. E. Deming. Quality meant everything in Japan, whereas in the United States it wasn't even on the table yet.

By the early 1970s, Japan had also gained a foothold in the American automotive market. With the 1973 Arab oil embargo boosting demand for fuel-efficient vehicles, by the end of the decade millions of Americans had sampled Japanese-made goods, and they liked them—because they worked.

Phase Two: The Rise of a New Values System
Throughout the 1970s, American consumers, flush with money, began to expect more from the products they purchased. A new set of values was born: The worry over quantity (can I get one?) shifted to quality (can I get a good one?).

This new value wasn't limited to consumers; it spread throughout the supply chain. Manufacturers realized that the quality of their products was only as good as the quality of their parts, so they began to use quality as a key buying guideline in dealing with their suppliers.

For example, electronics company Motorola now required that all its suppliers meet minimum quality specifications to make a bid for an order, declaring that if suppliers weren't planning on competing for the national quality award in Japan, they would lose Motorola's business. Likewise, Toyota told more than fifty American and Canadian auto parts suppliers that quality, not price, would be the basis of competition for its business.

Phase Three: The Arrival of the Innovators
Even though the American war machine created high-quality bullets and planes, the country's commercial sector couldn't get quality right. American companies suffered from high defect rates, while the Japanese were perfecting quality in electronics, home appliances, and compact cars. Their defect ratios were so low that, in many cases, Japanese manufacturers were one hundred times more efficient at producing defect-free products than their American rivals.

Furthermore, the Japanese had a singular management system

that required their leaders to manage for quality using statistical controls, not just inspections, as the Americans were doing at the time.

Still, a handful of innovative American companies embraced the quality movement early on and prospered. At the Nashua Corporation, a New Hampshire–based office and computer supply manufacturer, CEO Bill Conway made quality the defining element of his leadership style and convinced shareholders and investors to give his plan a chance. Conway turned his company into a quality leader in the computer memory disk market at a time when mighty Xerox and 3M had to exit the market altogether.

Another example of a quality-centered U.S. company is FedEx, which won the first Malcolm Baldrige National Quality Award for service in 1990. Founder and CEO Fred Smith was deeply committed to cutting-edge information technology to ensure reliability levels.

Phase Four: Disruption
The mid-to-late 1970s marked a bloodbath in the American economy. The Japanese took market share from American companies in every durable industry, including radios, televisions, personal gadgets, business machines, cars, and home appliances.

In 1950, the United States' auto and electronics makers owned almost 100 percent of domestic market share. By the end of the 1970s, Detroit had lost a quarter of its domestic market share to Japan. Likewise, the American computer industry lost 40 percent of its domestic market share during the same period. The machine tooling, personal electronics, and business machines sectors fared similarly.

In a classic example of innovators disrupting markets with little resistance from the incumbents, executives at most American companies didn't respond to Japan's initial success; instead, they acted as if they were waiting it out, like a bad storm—but the storm never ended.

Seven years later, *BusinessWeek* summed up the carnage: "Quality. Remember it? American manufacturing has slumped a long way from the glory days of the 1950s and 1960s when 'Made in U.S.A.' proudly stood for the best that industry could turn out. . . . While the Japanese were developing remarkably higher standards for a whole host of products, from consumer electronics to cars and machine tools, many U.S. managers were smugly dozing at the switch. Now, aside from aerospace and agriculture, there are few markets left where the U.S. carries its own weight in international trade. For American industry, the message is simple. Get better or get beat."

Phase Five: The New Order
America finally began to get the message, and major companies now hired the same consultants who had taught Japan about quality, including Deming. These companies reduced their defects, improved their quality, and regained competitiveness with the Japanese in most categories except for the auto industry, where Japan's early-mover advantage in quality had picked up too much steam.

As in any business revolution, the new values and innovations infected the entire U. S. economy. The quality revolution didn't stop at products; it spread to services, as organizations such as health care providers and phone companies were held to standards of quality, from billing to customer support.

Furthermore, American consumers and corporate purchasing agents have continued to raise the bar on what is considered high quality, pushing all companies to improve continually and to keep up with market leaders or face a loss in market share. Such is the nature of a new order: It permanently changes the rules and requirements of business.

Business revolutions are always around the corner, usually spurred by changing times, emerging values, and innovative companies that are reacting to up-and-coming market opportunities.

One company responding to the new revolution is the Finnish phone maker Nokia. In 2007, after giving a talk at a company conference, I spent time with several of its executives, exchanging ideas on business trends and strategy.

When I asked them what their major strategic initiatives during the 1980s and 1990s were, they responded, "Quality, quality, and quality!" Much like Motorola, Nokia created an aggressive program to reduce defects in manufacturing and improve the user experience through improved design.

But in a discussion about the company's strategic initiative for the coming century, they now replied, "Corporate responsibility."

One of Nokia's most remarkable initiatives is Helping Hands, a community improvement program in which employees are given two days a year to pursue any community-based initiative that matters to them. In some countries, Nokia team members choose educational outreach programs to help the unemployed find access to better jobs. In other countries, Nokia employees rebuild villages and towns impacted by natural disasters and disease. The Nokia executives also listed e-waste, sustainability, and disaster relief as key efforts in which they were investing over the next few years.

On the other hand, another telecommunications company where I recently spoke is sitting out this revolution—at least, so far. When I talked to one of its generals last year at a leadership event, he told me that corporate social responsibility was a distraction from the ongoing battle for quality and price.

"In ten years," he said, "nobody will care about the environment

or community service. They'll care about themselves and the price of
my handsets."

The former company has gained market share and talent over the
course of each passing year. The latter has suffered financial shortfalls, lost its position as a leader in the industry, and recently laid off
thousands of workers in an effort to cut losses.

Which kind of company do you want to be in the Responsibility
Revolution?

3

Phase One:
A Change in Circumstances

B race yourself.

Changes are coming that will threaten the stability of both your company and your industry. The world at work will never be the same. The barbarians (or the cavalry, depending on your point of view) are organized, mobilized, and on the move. In the immortal words of Bob Dylan, "A hard rain's a-gonna fall."

Even as you read this book, the Responsibility Revolution is under way. It is following the same blueprint as the Quality Revolution, and it is starting to disrupt the business landscape in an even more dramatic way.

As mentioned in the first chapter, the Responsibility Revolution is a broad-based movement of people and companies taking a disruptive approach to making a difference—contributing to our quality of life, locally and globally, for current and future generations.

Making a living and making a profit are not enough for these people. Armed with wealth, knowledge, and talent, they are using their money and time as levers to pressure companies to change their ways. They believe business possesses the money, technology, people, and power to fix the problems of today's world.

To many consumers and shareholders, the new profit-and-loss

statement is the social profit-and-loss. If you were to configure this P&L on behalf of your company, it would comprise a two-column list, with the left column designating social profit and the right column social loss. For example, a company's education program to lift local graduation rates goes into the social profit column. A company's factory waste contaminating local groundwater falls into the social loss column.

In the end, the items in the social profits column must significantly exceed those in the social loss column to gain public trust. Concerned consumers and citizens will punish you for social losses.

Over the next few years, this way of thinking will shake up every industry, including yours. You may face competitors so socially efficient that they enjoy an operating cost advantage over you. Already, revolutionary companies are beginning to see side benefits from socially valuable programs: cost savings, improvements in productivity, and areas for revenue growth.

If you've sent a child to college in the last few years, chances are good that you've visited the home furnishings store IKEA. Why not? The store offers great products at remarkable prices. How do they do it? Unlike Wal-Mart, which built a cost advantage through volume purchasing, IKEA cuts costs through social efficiency. In an effort to squeeze environmental costs and energy consumption out of their business operations, the company started an eco-friendly flat-packaging program several years ago. The program quickly became a point of pride among IKEA's employees as the company worked to find new ways to improve the fill-rate of each box that leaves the store.

According to Daniel Esty and Andrew Winston in their book *Green to Gold*, "That smart packing saves up to 15 percent on fuel per item—a striking Eco-Advantage—and it inspires workers [at IKEA] to stretch the envelope even more."

Not surprisingly, IKEA ranked as one of the five most productive companies in the world in a 2002 study commissioned by author Jason Jennings.

This same story is playing out in the world of industrial carpets, autos, computers, toys, health care, and so on. The ground is already shaking as you read this book, the signs of disruption rumbling up like temblors. The five phases of the Responsibility Revolution are already playing themselves out, as follows:

The first change in the landscape of modern life centers on a dramatic boost in information.

Life before the Internet offered only a few information sources: the Yellow Pages, newspapers, magazines, television news, and local libraries. Word of mouth tended to be limited by the size of our social circles, which were invariably small.

Today, the Internet has given users an abundance of alternatives. If you don't like the products at your local store, log on to the Web and exponentially increase your selection. If the Sunday paper doesn't provide you enough job possibilities, search any of dozens of job sites. If you need more information about a product than the company offers, check out the blogs, bulletin boards, and chat rooms.

Barriers to information flow are falling. There is no editorial control over most of the Web's content. There is no space limitation on a blog or a viral e-mail. Nothing is private in the new world of total information. Word-of-mouse is now limited only by the appetite of the online community for information on the subject. Any decision can be researched, discussed, and compared against any alternative. Over time, information will become even more useful, more available, and more ubiquitous as innovations in wireless phones, kiosk technology, and pervasive computing continue.

The second context change has to do with our perceived sense of safety and security. The great majority of media information is negative, from terrorist threats to natural disaster to unthinkable crime. While such events have always existed, today's media deliver them fast, raw, and in real time, thanks to satellite technology.

On one single day, April 16, 2007, a lone gunman killed more than thirty people at Virginia Tech and mailed a video filled with rants and rage to NBC, which then distributed it to other networks; they were soon playing it repeatedly. Meanwhile, the killer's manifesto spread like wildfire on the Internet, eventually reaching more than a billion people via all forms of media.

The third major change in the context of modern life is our distrust of the world's major corporations.

Business news was once relegated to the back sections of the newspapers. Today corporate scandals take center stage in the media, making the business pages resemble the police blotter. Leaders at major companies such as Enron, WorldCom, HealthSouth, AIG, Fannie Mae, and Merck were caught cheating, lying, or stealing.

Accounting scandals involving the backdating of stock options at dozens of companies have further tainted business. In a late-2004 poll, only 14 percent of average Americans said that they believed that "what was good for business was good for most Americans." Eight years previously, the same poll found twice as many econo-optimists.

Finally, the environment crisis has gained urgency from virtually every quarter. Helping to lead this charge has been former Vice President Al Gore, who presented the case in his Academy Award–winning documentary, *An Inconvenient Truth*; Gore's book of the same name was an enormous bestseller. By 2006, the general public's attitude had shifted from skepticism to belief; according to Jem Bendell, founder of the Lifeworth research organization, the concept began "to be understood as a humanitarian emergency."

In 2007, leading youth trends researchers at the Intelligence

Group found that global warming was the number one concern for respondents under the age of forty, as cited in their *Cassandra Report*.

A great many changes have rattled our social atmosphere. At the same time as we've been bestowed information-based empowerment, we've also been robbed of our ability to guarantee a safe future for our children. Anyone born in the tornado alley that is West Texas, as I was, understands what happens during an onslaught of diverse changes in the atmosphere. You get a storm. The more dramatic the collision of elements, the worse the storm—like the 1970 Lubbock tornado that leveled everything in its path.

Think of the positive changes mentioned as a warm air flow of opportunity that has swept through our psyche and lifted our spirits. Imagine the disturbing changes as a cold air of dread that has depressed our souls. The convergence of these two extremes has created an environment similar to what happens when high- and low-pressure fronts collide in the sky. The rapid changes in the atmosphere of daily life are brewing a major social storm.

4

Phase Two:
The Rise of a New Value System

Darren Glover is a father of two, a college graduate, and a district sales manager for a retail furniture chain in Maryland. Fifteen years ago, when he shopped at the grocery store, he read product labels solely for health information.

Today, Darren does more than read labels. He researches companies on the Internet to learn their level of social responsibility. Darren moved from worrying about his own health to the health of the workers who were part of the product's production cycle.

Ten years ago, Darren scrutinized employment opportunities on the basis of salary and benefits. Today, he screens a company first for sustainability, social outreach, and treatment of the employees.

Seven years ago, Darren instructed his financial advisor to invest his money to make a minimum annual financial return. Today, he invests in companies the same way he buys products and considers career opportunities—with the world in mind. The vast majority of his investment portfolio is weighted in socially responsible investment funds (SRIs).

In an increasingly interconnected world, Darren sees himself as more than just an individual; his questions and concerns involve more than just himself and his family—they include the plight of people living in distant lands and the fate of future generations. Darren is a member of a new generation: the Them Generation.

Millions of adult Americans like Darren possess a new set of priorities in their personal and professional lives. They want their lives to make a difference to the world.

Michael Adams, in his bestselling book *American Backlash: The Untold Story of Social Change in the United States*, explains: "For most of history the pace of change for us humans culturally and technologically, and certainly spiritually, can only be described as glacial. . . . Not so in today's rapid world . . . of invention and cultural convergence, where knowledge is discovered so rapidly it can double within half a single generation."

How have the recent experiences in Phase One influenced our values?

Change One: The Information Boom

An abundance of information empowers people to become highly selective about companies with whom they choose to do business. Why settle for a product that isn't green, or a job at a company filled with unhappy employees, or buy stock in a conglomerate that mistreats its overseas workers? ThemGeners routinely use the latest online tools to screen for social responsibility and find alternatives.

A 2006 survey conducted by the public relations firm Fleishman-Hillard and the National Consumers League found that "58 percent [of Americans] say that because of the increased availability of online resources and information, they are more informed about companies' records for social responsibility than they were a few years ago."

In the past, information was tightly controlled by business. The information that did trickle down drove social activism, whether it came in the form of a movie such as *The China Syndrome* or a news exposé, like *60 Minutes'* report on a company dumping chemicals into New York's Hudson River.

Today, the trickle has expanded into a gushing torrent of information about any company or, for that matter, any executive. No company is too sacred to discuss. Bulletin board participants seek the truth in a no-holds-barred conversation. The result is a greater level of transparency. And when people discover mischief, they mobilize against it.

The Internet Effect allows more people to be socially conscious. Technology leads to the dispersion of information, and information, in turn, leads to a higher level of social accountability for all.

Change Two: A Threat to Security and Safety
Most people who have suffered through traumatic experiences emerge with a new perspective on life, as well as new priorities. Of all of the recent events that have jarred America, the terrorist tragedies of September 11 stand out as the most powerful.

As Harvard professor Robert Putnam writes in his book *Bowling Alone: The Collapse and Revival of American Community*: "Why would the 2001 terrorist attacks affect this generation so? . . . The attacks and their aftermath demonstrated that our fates are highly interdependent. We learned that we need to—and can—depend on the kindness of strangers who happen to be near us in a plane, office building or subway."

Leading brand-research firm Cone Inc. conducted a study in late 2001 and early 2002 to determine how the tragedies have translated to attitudes and behavior. The researchers concluded that "armed with a heightened expectation of corporate citizenship that was inspired by the national tragedy, Americans as investors, consumers and employees say they are willing to use their individual power to *punish* those companies that do not share their values."

Change Three: Scandals

The number of corporate flameouts between 2000 and 2003 was unprecedented. Tens of thousands of families lost their pensions or investments when Enron collapsed, and the entire economy felt the ripple effect in the resulting 2002 stock market swoon.

The media circus that surrounded these events made the scandals a daily part of our lives and led to a new set of values. The Cone study found that "89 percent of Americans say that in light of the Enron collapse and WorldCom financial situation, it is more important than ever for companies to be socially responsible."

So far, the public doesn't think that companies are doing a good enough job in that arena. In the 2006 Fleishman-Hillard survey, three out of four Americans give U.S. companies "less-than-high marks" in the area of operating in a socially responsible manner.

And the bar is continually being raised. In a 2006 *Harvard Business Review* article, Roger Martin, dean of the Rotman School of Management at the University of Toronto, pointed out, "What used to be considered leading and enlightened social or environmental practices . . . are now considered to be the entry-level ante for a social license to operate."

Change Four: The Environmental Crisis

Now that skepticism about global warming has given way to belief, many of us have made the environment a top priority. But none has embraced it more than today's youth, raised on recycling and save-the-planet campaigns, and now poised to spring into action. As James Gustave Speth, dean of Yale University's School of Forestry and Environment Studies, told *Newsweek* in 2007: "We're on the verge of a sea change in young people's engagement with climate and other environment issues."

A 2007 Gallup poll showed that 44 percent of those between

eighteen and thirty-four strongly believe we "need to take immediate, drastic action on the environment." (This belief is shared by 38 percent of the adults between thirty-five and fifty-four, and 33 percent of adults fifty-five and older.)

Millions of citizens sense a profound urgency to act. They chide one another for using too much energy. They scrutinize products to see if they are good or bad for the environment. They write letters to companies, as well as to politicians. They bring the issue up at the dinner table with their relatives. In the same *Newsweek* story, Paul Hawken, author of *The Ecology of Commerce*, said that over and over he heard a variation on the same story: "CEO's daughter comes home from college and says, 'Dad, we can't be that stupid.' "

In consumer circles, disposable products are out and reusable ones are in. Synthetic is cold and organic is hot. At the grocery store, shoppers ask clerks where products were manufactured and under what conditions. If they don't like the answers, they take their business elsewhere.

ThemGeners have a different definition of product quality; it's based not on look, feel, or durability, but sustainability and fairness—to them, high quality means high quality for the planet.

When values change, so do the rules we apply to everyday situations. They form the criteria by which we allocate resources, and we apply these beliefs to all facets of our lives.

Following are three key areas in which we decide how to allocate our personal resources: how we buy, where we work, and where we invest.

How We Buy

The market for values-driven commerce has grown exponentially over the last decade. Cone, along with the Roper polling organization, has been researching consumer trends along social responsibility lines since 1997. In its 1999 survey, the company found that 65 percent of American consumers would be willing to switch from one brand to another, equal in quality and price, if it were associated with a good cause.

In 2000, the *New York Times* reported that the market for values-driven commerce, including eco-friendly, organic, and fair-trade products, had grown to almost a quarter of a trillion dollars and was continuing to surge by double digits with each passing year.

Not only were customers seeking out products that reflected their values, they stood ready to stop using those that didn't—the Cone 2002 Corporate Citizen Study found that 76 percent of consumers would boycott a company if they discovered it has practiced negative corporate citizenship (30 percent higher than the company's 1999 results). Researchers also found that the number of respondents willing to switch to a product from a more socially responsible provider (price and quality being equal) had jumped to 84 percent—a 50 percent increase from 1999.

With each passing year, marketers find that significantly greater portions of the population have developed new values for what they purchase. Consider the market for green products: In 2005, research conducted by the Natural Marketing Institute in conjunction with author and sociology researcher Paul H. Ray identified a new market called LOHAS (lifestyles of health and sustainability).

According to the study, 63 million adult Americans are LOHAS consumers and spend almost one half of a trillion dollars annually.

Unlike previous findings, in which consumers showed a willingness to switch to a socially good company when price was roughly equal, Paul Ray's study found that even though "they are not necessarily wealthier than other Americans, [LOHAS] have proven themselves willing to spend up to an astounding 20 percent premium on clean, green products over the nonsustainable alternatives."

A clear example of such price elasticity in action shows up in a 2005 study sponsored by *Book Tech* magazine and administered by the Green Press Initiative, a nonprofit research organization serving book and magazine publishers. It found that 80 percent of book and magazine buyers would pay more for products printed on recycled paper; a significant portion (42 percent) would even pay a dollar more per book, or seventy-five cents more per magazine.

Millions of the younger ThemGeners are heavily influenced by a company's social track record when they make a purchase. In 2006, leading youth-marketing research company Alloy Media partnered with Harris Interactive to measure how college students make their purchasing decisions. According to the report, "In the eyes of college students, factors that make a good employer also make desirable products. This research shows that college students rank social responsibility higher than celebrity endorsements as factors in their choice of consumer brands. Some 33 percent of the respondents say they prefer brands known for involvement with not-for-profit causes, community activism or environmentally friendly practices."

Where We Work

As a young adult in the 1980s, I looked at each job opportunity through an economic lens. How much did it pay? What were the benefits? How secure was this job?

I wasn't alone; most of us defined the quality of a job offer financially. Today things are different. ThemGeners want to work for a company with a good social track record.

In 1997, *BusinessWeek* joined forces with Net Impact, a nonprofit organization comprising thousands of young business leaders, to study how MBAs decide among competing job offers. After interviewing several thousand MBA students, researchers found that 50 percent would accept a smaller salary to work at a company that was very socially responsible, while 43 percent would not work for a company that failed to practice social responsibility.

(Such sentiments aren't limited to MBAs. In the 2000 National Business Ethics Survey, an annual research project conducted by the Ethics Resource Center, 75 percent of employees said that "an organization's concern for ethics and doing the right thing was an important reason for continuing to work there.")

The labor consulting firm DBM's survey of human resource and career-placement professionals in North America and Europe found that 82 percent of respondents cite corporate leadership ethics as very important to job seekers. DBM president Tom Silveri remarked, "We're seeing a response to the ethical and corporate governance issues that have recently hampered the U.S. market. Job seekers are putting more time into researching prospective employers before making a decision on a new job. Globally, employers are being held to the highest of standards by current and future employees."

In its 2002 Corporate Citizenship study, Cone Inc. noted a surge of social screening by job candidates. In its survey, 77 percent of respondents indicated that "a company's commitment to social issues is important when I decide where to work." This figure was 80 percent higher than the findings in Cone Inc.'s spring 2001 survey, taken before the Enron collapse and the events of September 11.

This same survey found that 80 percent would refuse to take a job at a company they found lacking in social responsibility.

One way to see which businesses are poised for future success is to track the flow of business school graduates, based on their requirements of potential employers. A 2003 Stanford Graduate School of Business study of almost one thousand graduating MBAs at the nation's top ten schools, conducted by professors David Montgomery and Catherine Ramus, found that "97 percent of the MBAs . . . said they were willing to forgo financial benefits to work for an organization with a better reputation for corporate social responsibility and ethics."

The study defined exactly how much the MBAs would forgo: 14 percent of salary, which means that if an MBA student received a $200,000-per-year offer from Dunkin' Donuts and a competing offer of $172,000 from Starbucks, he or she might well choose the latter.

I pick this example because, historically, Starbucks pays a little less to its executives than many of its competitors, yet wins the ongoing battles for executive talent. Craig Weatherup, the former CEO at Pepsi Bottling Group, sits on Starbucks' board and has observed many recruitment campaigns to land top candidates. In a recent interview for *CRO*, an executive recruiting publication, he said, "In terms of recruiting an executive to Starbucks, there is no question that corporate social responsibility is a tie-breaker."

Even at the non-executive or non-MBA level, having a good social reputation will attract talent. Robert Morgan, former CEO of global staffing firm Spherion, said in an interview in *Workforce Management* that "a reputation for social responsibility can often be the determining factor when a candidate is deciding between two or three companies."

As early as 2002, recruiting and placement professionals began to realize that to compete, their client companies would need to bolster their social compensation plans. (A social comp plan includes make-a-difference opportunities for each employee, along with a salary and benefits package; offering time off to serve the community, or matching employee contributions to a foundation, are examples of such perks.)

In 2006, a Cone Inc. study of teens and twentysomethings found that the preference for socially valuable employers was holding strong. Eight of ten respondents indicated that they wanted to work for a company that cares about its impact on society.

The rules for attracting talent have changed—cash is no longer king. Neither the quality of your products nor the price of your stocks will bring in the best and the brightest. With each passing year, job seekers are becoming more socially focused, asking themselves: How can I use my talent to make a difference?

How We Invest

Traditionally, investments such as stocks and bonds were a means of building financial wealth and security. Over the last twenty-five years, however, many investors have changed their outlook on the purpose of their investments. They still want to see their dollars producing returns, but they also want those returns to be as good for the world as for their nest egg.

Socially responsible investing (SRI) is the practice of including social along with financial criteria when choosing an investment. Investors are practicing SRI when they consider a potential investment's current and prospective impact on communities, the environment, and society at large.

Investors and investment managers practice SRI in three ways. The first is to invest in social funds. These funds operate like traditional mutual funds, except that they institute social screens, which bar certain types of companies such as cigarette manufacturers and major polluters, and seek out those with exceptional social performance, such as sustainability policies, community investments, or awards for being great companies to work for. Such funds have strict rules about who can or cannot be included, and are often arranged thematically by social benefit, such as Green Funds, Community Funds, and so on.

The second type of SRI is practiced by investment managers who oversee traditional mutual funds or equity funds that aren't designed with a social theme per se. While such funds are geared mainly to produce a financial return, the fund manager uses social criteria alongside traditional criteria to evaluate and select investments.

The third type of SRI is practiced through shareholder activism, in which an investor or fund manager takes a position in a company explicitly to wield influence as an owner. For example, an investor might buy Exxon stock in order to appear at the annual shareholders' meeting and speak out against the company's lack of investment in alternative energy. Or a fund manager might author a resolution requiring one of his holdings to report on efforts to improve the quality of life of suppliers in developing countries.

Socially responsible investment isn't new to America—in the early 1800s, Quakers refused to invest in any company associated with slavery. But it remained an underdeveloped part of the investment community until the 1971 birth of the Pax World Fund. In protest against the Vietnam War, Pax avoided any companies with ties to the military.

A year later, the Dreyfus Corporation launched the Third Century Fund, which excluded any companies doing business in South Africa due to its apartheid policies. This fund also sought out companies with good records for employment opportunities and safety.

In 1982, the Calvert Group initiated the Calvert Money Market Portfolio and within fifteen years was offering five different funds arranged around various social criteria to meet investor preferences.

The social funds sector got another boost in 1999 when Dow Jones created the Dow Jones Sustainability Index (DJSI) series of funds that screened companies for environmental and socially sustainable performance. As more funds were added to the market mix, traditional fund managers began to see the long-term benefit of socially screening investments.

In a survey conducted in 1999 for the Calvert Group by research firm Yankelovich, this rise in credibility was demonstrated by a marked increase (from one-third to almost half) in the number of investors who believed that SRIs performed as well as or better than the general market.

Between the launch of Pax World in 1971 and the end of 2001, assets in socially screened mutual funds jumped from $150 million to more than $100 billion—a 6,800 percent increase, compared with a 1,350 percent increase for mutual funds in general.

By the end of 2003, social funds topped $150 billion in assets. At the same time, more than $2 trillion of investment assets were socially screened by mainstream fund managers, representing one out of every ten dollars invested in the United States. At this point, traditional just-for-profit stock pickers started to realize that investors were looking at more than dollars and cents in the companies they held.

In the last few years, SRIs have found still more ways to gobble up investment dollars. One area of growth is community investing, in which a fund is created to bolster a specific community with schools, hospitals, and small business loans. In less than a decade, community investment funds have quadrupled in size, from less than $4 billion to almost $20 billion.

These socially mindful investors are acting more like owners than traders or gamblers, creating a radically new environment in which to operate. For the corporate world, as investors demand more than profits, even a company that performs well financially may find its stock price plummeting if it fails to meet social responsibility metrics.

In one of my favorite books, *The Cluetrain Manifesto*, marketing savants Christopher Locke, Rick Levine, Doc Searls, and David Weinberger observed, "Markets are nothing more than conversations. . . . The first markets were filled with people, not abstractions or statistical aggregates: they were the places where supply met demand with a firm handshake. Buyers and sellers looked each other in the eyes, met and connected."

Today's social value marketplace works like this, too: A conversation between coffee drinkers about where their coffee beans come from, and how much the employees at that source are paid, fuels the demand for coffee produced by workers who earn a reasonable wage. As the drinkers continue to talk, they discover that the reason workers in South America are so underpaid is that the multinational coffee merchants are paying unfairly low prices for the coffee beans, leaving little to pay the workers. When the coffee drinkers convey their feelings to their coffee providers, they motivate them to pay a fair price for a pound of beans and give them what they want: social justice in a cup.

As more drinkers enter the conversation between customer and company, the greater a new opportunity grows for the coffee providers. This opportunity is called the new market for fair-trade coffee. As the discussion continues, the market grows. According to data gathered in 2004 by the National Coffee Association, "Awareness of fair-trade coffee among U.S. drinkers has risen to 12 percent in 2004, up from 7 percent in 2003, and purchases among those aware have risen to 45 percent from 38 percent."

Similar conversations take place in the job marketplace. For example, a top candidate and a hiring official discuss a career that is meaningful and socially valuable. The candidate makes it clear that he will choose the job offer that best delivers this benefit, even if wages are lower. As the hiring official has more of these conversations with other job seekers, she realizes that her company isn't prepared to meet this demand. This realization leads to discussions inside the company on how to design jobs that offer such benefits.

As these dialogues reach senior management, executives seek out ways the company can make a more significant social contribution. Eventually, as the desire for meaningful work is met with job opportunities that offer a chance to help society *and* make a wage, the market for meaningful work emerges.

Conversations about new values create new markets, replete with prospective buyers and the other essential ingredient: companies willing to play in this new space.

As you will soon see, some people in the business world are great conversation partners. They station themselves at the front lines of the business battle, listen in, and offer their two cents' worth. From this form of conversation comes innovation.

5

Phase Three:
The Arrival of the Innovators

The rise in social values goes beyond changing how people buy, take jobs, or invest. It invades the very core of how people do business. Remember, ThemGeners come in all ages and from all walks of life. Many of them work inside the system, where they adapt their existing companies to serve these new values, while others start new companies based on social missions rather than financial ones.

These people are reinventing how business is conducted. Sometimes they're serving markets that were previously underserved; at other times, they are setting out to create and fuel them. They play the role of spoiler to the old guard. Health enthusiasts create companies that offer nutritious, organic food—often because they can't find what they want on the market. Environmentalists build companies that improve the environment in ways that others don't, and make money as a result. Fair-trade advocates design their companies to ensure that farmworkers receive a living wage, education for their children, and an improving quality of life.

Such entrepreneurs are forming companies consistent with their values, from doing the right thing for their customers and employees to doing the right thing for the planet. Most of the time, when they start, they are the only companies in their space as they try to satisfy the values of a very small group of people. However, as often as not, these spaces expand as the number of customers grows.

In the Responsibility Revolution, the first wave of innovators are the pioneers—those people who arrived on the scene filled with ideas and energy before others even knew there was a scene. Billionaire entrepreneur and Dallas Mavericks owner Mark Cuban, for whom I worked at Broadcast.com, remarked that these pioneers "get a lot of arrows in their back for going first." It's often painful to chart new territory because there are no rules yet, and mistake after mistake is made.

But some people love a challenge, especially if solving it allows them to be first-to-market with a breakthrough product or service. When these pioneering innovators succeed, they fan the flames of a business revolution by finding a way to serve new values that the incumbent industry leaders had previously thought to be too difficult or too expensive. When they crack the code, they offer a new value proposition for the times.

Frequently, the pioneering innovators offer a value proposition that is not quite ready for prime time. The market for their vision is microscopic. Their products are often too expensive, too hard to find, or considered low quality by traditional standards. For what can seem like an endless amount of time, the market doesn't recognize the founder's innovation.

While each pioneering company starts off with a single visionary or a small group of founders, the leaders soon realize the company can't succeed without help from others. As the plot unfolds, dedicated employees, raving fans, and doting journalists help the pioneer find a traction point and defy the odds by making a profit.

Eventually, as the market for socially responsible products and services expands, the pioneer achieves enough size and scale to offer products or services that are as affordable and high quality as they are innovative.

In researching this book, I've interviewed countless business leaders, looking for stories of pioneering innovators who chose to add social value before a market existed. Among the most exemplary is Horst Rechelbacher, founder of the personal-care products company Aveda.

Horst (who goes only by his first name) was born in Austria in 1941. His mother dispensed medicines at an apothecary and concocted natural teas, tonics, and extracts for ailing customers. His father, a shoemaker, designed custom shoes out of wood.

Due to dyslexia, Horst wasn't a good student. His teachers encouraged him to pursue a trade, so he dropped out of school and found a job at a hair salon. He started out as a cleaner, but at age fourteen became apprenticed to a hairstylist.

Horst's skill impressed his boss, who sent Horst to numerous competitions; by 1958, he'd won two junior national hairstyling championships. Many European championships followed, and soon Horst was invited to the United States to perform in national hair shows.

In 1964, after Horst had performed in a Minneapolis hair show, his car was violently rear-ended by a drunk driver. Sustaining numerous injuries from the accident, including a broken back, Horst soon piled up more than $20,000 in hospital bills. Hospital administrators then seized his passport, fearing he'd flee back to Europe without paying his bill, so Horst went to work as a stylist at a local salon. Within a year, a banker client gave him a loan to start his own salon, Horst & Friends, which soon became one of the city's most successful.

At this point, Horst became interested in hair-care products, conferring with a chemist friend and developing his own brand of hair spray, a strong aerosol polyvinyl chloride (PVC)–based product. The product performed better, had a slightly less offensive smell, and required less spray to hold hair than other sprays.

Shortly thereafter, Horst's mother voiced her disapproval of his career because she found the salon experience unhealthy: PVC-based hair sprays and certain hair products are potential causes of lung cancer, from which several of Horst's friends later died.

Horst's own health was deteriorating; his mother nursed him back to vitality with herbal remedies, reintroducing him to nature's solutions. Inspired, Horst soon concocted new plant-based products; his first breakthrough was a clove-based shampoo.

In 1967, after hearing a moving lecture by an Indian researcher and yogi, Horst spent six months in the Himalayas studying Ayurveda (the ancient Indian system of preventative health care), meeting with local scientists and shamans, and deepening his connection with nature's medicine chest. These travels convinced him that business had to be in harmony with nature. Realizing that the hair-care industry wasn't sustainable—most of its ingredients were in limited supply and ate up precious natural resources—he tackled the puzzle of creating care products that were as good for the environment as they were for the human body.

By 1978, Horst had developed an idea for a company that included concept salons, beauty academies, and a full line of personal-care products made entirely of plants and essential oils. After returning to India to further his Ayurveda training, he formed his company, Aveda, Sanskrit for "all nature's knowledge."

Horst was convinced he could create plant-based hair-care

products that would outperform chemical-based competitors. His initial mission statement read: "Our mission at Aveda is to care for the world we live in, from the products we make to the ways in which we give back to society."

In the beginning, Aveda struggled to gather distribution and make word-of-mouth sales; neither salon owners nor customers seemed concerned about hair products' health or environmental implications. But Horst had faith the market would grow, and by 1991, Aveda was clearing more than $50 million in annual revenue and gaining market momentum.

As one of the earliest adopters of sustainability, Horst was invited to speak at the 1992 Earth Summit in Rio de Janeiro. A year later, he returned to Brazil to meet with leaders from local tribes to discuss possible partnerships synergistic with his product vision and the needs of indigenous people.

Back in Minnesota, Aveda chemists discovered that uruku, a rain forest plant, contained a reddish-brown pigment useful in makeup. This discovery gave Horst a basis for a partnership with the Brazilian tribesmen. He lived among them for several days, observing their daily rituals and habits. Finally, he decided to pursue a business arrangement with the Yawanawa tribe; his company partnered with them to take a clear-cut piece of land and build a village called Nova Esperanca, or New Hope, where they gathered and transplanted over a quarter million seedlings of uruku for Aveda's product line. The company now had an endless supply of low-cost pigment and the tribespeople had an alternative income source to selling logging rights to the remaining rain forest.

Horst was also turning evangelical about the power of natural, nonpoisonous business practices. He eliminated all but 5 percent of petrochemical and synthetic ingredients in his product line; he ensured the bottles in which the cosmetics were sold were composed of almost 50 percent recycled plastic; he had his R&D team toil away at an innovation to replace the plastic with corn and sugar-beet-based packaging that could be reused as compost to grow plants.

Horst's dream was to infect his competitors and his industry, so he also introduced a revolutionary line of plant-based fragrances to tackle another problem: synthetic fragrances, which he believed were poison. The product, dubbed Love Pure-Fume, was an immediate cult hit.

Three events in 1997 changed the course of the company's history. First, Aveda discovered that a key ingredient of Love Pure-Fume, sandalwood oil, had been stolen from forests in East India; the sourcing of the product wasn't sustainable and would eventually lead to deforestation. The company immediately ceased production of the fragrance, took the product off the shelves, and sought out a socially responsible source for sandalwood. Love Pure-Fume didn't return for five years, until a sustainable source was found in Australia.

The second major event was Horst's realization that if Aveda were to compete globally, it would have to go public. Absent significant resources, the firm couldn't gain market share from its chemical competitors or the new crop of natural products from other companies he had inspired.

Third, Horst had a chance meeting with Leonard Lauder, the chairman of cosmetics conglomerate Estée Lauder, who was interested in acquiring Aveda to serve as the high-end, high-purpose brand in the Estée empire. Horst trusted Lauder, who assured him that Aveda's mission would remain intact. Horst was also convinced that by placing Aveda inside Estée Lauder as its crown jewel, he might influence his company's new parent. The same year, Lauder purchased Aveda for $300 million in cash. Horst stepped down from his role as CEO but remained as a consultant on the Aveda board after the acquisition.

During this time, Estée Lauder searched for a new leader for Aveda—one who could combine business skills with the same values Horst had infused into the company. Two years later, Dominique Conseil, a Frenchman who'd been running L'Oréal's business in Japan, was given the job.

When Conseil took up residence at the corporate headquarters in late 2000, he picked up where the founder had left off: the mission, not the money. In 2001, Conseil's Aveda launched a joint venture with Rare, an American-based conservation consulting company, and the Global Greengrants Fund to empower indigenous people to become economically self-sufficient without sacrificing natural resources. (It was Conseil who, in 2002, struck a deal with an Australian tribe for sandalwood and relaunched Love Pure-Fume.)

Conseil continued to leverage relationships with customers and suppliers to raise consciousness. In 2004, retail stores and salons that sold Aveda products expanded their Earth Day promotions to an entire Earth Month. And the company required suppliers to increase the level of postconsumer content in their bottles and packaging.

Most notably, the head of Aveda's packaging development group issued a challenge to Wheaton Plastics (now ALCAN) to increase the postconsumer content of its hair-care product bottles from 45 to 80 percent. Wheaton delivered the required ratio, saved Aveda a million dollars in shipping costs (thanks to dramatically reduced bottle weight), and helped the company spare 140 million tons of unsustainable virgin plastic material.

ALCAN took this idea to other product manufacturers, along with the projected cost savings, and helped other companies see the Aveda way.

At the same time, Aveda's marketing group challenged their print advertising suppliers to print on partially recycled paper or lose its business. By the end of 2003, Aveda had announced it would buy ads only in publications that had at least 10 percent post-consumer recycled content. Meanwhile, *Yoga Journal* silently switched from 10 percent recycled to 100 percent virgin paper in July of 2004. When Aveda ad buyers got wind of this, they stopped advertising in the magazine. By the November 2004 issue, *Yoga Journal* had returned to using partially recycled paper.

Next, Aveda wanted to make an impression on one of the world's biggest publishers, Time Inc. Aveda ad managers asked magazines to fill out sustainability surveys to determine with whom they would advertise, in the process educating publishers about the contribution of publishing to global warming. Inspired by this dialogue, Time Inc. participated in a 2006 study that measured the carbon emissions created by the company's *Time* and *In Style* magazines. The study revealed that a single paper mill Time Inc. used was responsible for almost two-thirds of the company's total carbon emissions. The corporation then issued an edict that all paper suppliers must reduce their greenhouse-gas emissions by 20 percent by 2012.

Aveda educated its customers too; a 2005 survey had revealed that 56 percent of Aveda customers were aware of the company's mission and wanted to participate. When Aveda launched a radical new concept for lipstick, refillable cardboard lipstick shells, these customers responded favorably. According to Conseil, consumers bought not just one refillable case for three lipsticks as suggested, they bought one for six. And they told their friends, becoming a central part of Aveda's ongoing marketing program.

Since Aveda's acquisition by Estée Lauder in 1997, the annual revenues have grown four times, a rate significantly faster than that of almost all other leading consumer goods manufacturers. As Aveda grows, so does its influence.

———

Dozens of other innovators were taking the same journey to resolve the tension between business and society; I'd like to talk about two more of them, starting with Yvon Chouinard, president of the outdoor clothing and gear company Patagonia.

While Horst was learning the art and science of hair care, fourteen-year-old Yvon Chouinard was joining the Southern California Falconry Club, where he started rappelling down cliffs to reach remote falcon aeries. Chouinard soon became involved in the local climbing community, many of whose members were also part of the Sierra Club environmental group. Within a few years, Chouinard was tackling steep climbing challenges, such as the walls of Yosemite.

One of a climber's key tools is the piton, usually made of a soft iron, which was hammered into cliff faces, then left behind after one use. Not only wasteful, it was expensive: Climbing a steep rock required hundreds of piton placements.

After meeting a Swiss skier who had created his own reusable, hard-steel pitons, Chouinard decided to do the same. In 1957, he fashioned a blacksmith forge at his parents' house and made cast-iron, high-quality reusable pitons that he sold for $1.50 each. These pitons developed a cult following, and eight years later when demand had outstripped Chouinard's personal production capability, he partnered with a climbing buddy, a gifted engineer named Tom Frost. Together they designed a high-quality line of climbing tools. By the early 1970s, they had become the largest provider of climbing hardware in the United States.

Chouinard fell into the apparel side of the business by accident. While on a 1970 trip to Scotland, he bought a rugby shirt to wear while climbing. Back in California, other climbers wanted one too. So he imported a small batch from England, which immediately sold out. He then added the shirts to his product line and was soon in the apparel business, vending shirts, mittens, pants, and heavy-duty undergarments to outdoors lovers.

In 1973, realizing the need to create a brand, he named his company after one of the world's most beautiful places: Patagonia, in Argentina.

Chouinard never aspired to run a business. He always thought of himself as an adventurer first and a manufacturer/retailer second. His company's mission statement: "Build the best product, do no unnecessary harm, use business to inspire and implement solutions to the environmental crisis."

Patagonia pioneered several social innovations during this phase. In the mid-1980s, when downsizing was king, Patagonia was one of the first companies to offer free on-site day care. It subsidized high-quality food at its corporate cafeterias. Its corporate policy encouraged employees to take time off to go surfing when the waves were right. If an employee's child was sick, the parent was given paid leave to stay home. If an employee wanted to help a nonprofit environmental group, he or she was granted up to sixty days a year of paid leave to pursue it. Chouinard believed that a company could be generous to employees and afford them a lifestyle and a business life at the same time.

In 1986, Chouinard committed the company to what he called "The 1 Percent Solution," whereby 1 percent of all profits or 10 percent of sales (whichever is higher) is committed to wildlife preservation.

On the environmental front, Patagonia was one of the first catalog mail-order companies to use recycled paper. It also innovated production; for example, jacket fleece had always been derived from crude-oil products. Patagonia product developers found a way to produce a high-quality fleece using discarded soda-pop bottles instead. The product line, dubbed Synchilla (a play on the words synthetic and chinchilla), was an immediate success.

Inspired by the Synchilla line, in 1994, Chouinard instituted an environmental assessment of all materials used to produce the company's apparel line; he discovered that traditionally grown cotton was the biggest threat that Patagonia's products posed to the environment: 10 percent of all American pesticide chemicals were used to grow cotton. He gave his company less than two years to convert the entire Patagonia line into organic cotton; by 1996, the conversion was complete. Even though organic cotton could add as much as five dollars to the price of a polo shirt or a pair of chinos, Patagonia developed a small but growing market of organic-clothing enthusiasts.

By the end of the 1990s, Chouinard and his team were convinced that global warming was real. A sign was posted at its headquarters in Ventura, California: "There Is No Business to Be Done on a Dead Planet."

Patagonia leveraged all of its powers, from marketing to purchasing, to influence others to become involved in environmental initiatives. It dedicated valuable space in its mail-order catalog to educate and enlist customers to participate in campaigns from water conservation to stopping global warming. Patagonia buyers gave suppliers an ultimatum to improve their eco-efficiency. And as part of a partnership, Chouinard and his team counseled executives at Wal-Mart on topics ranging from organic cotton to recycling. By 2006, Wal-Mart had become the world's number one purchaser of organic cotton.

In 2001, Chouinard created a nonprofit membership organization, dubbed the "1 Percent for the Planet Alliance," to urge other companies to commit to the same give-back profit principles. As of 2007, almost five hundred companies had signed on, including tech giants Google and Salesforce.com. Collectively, these groups will contribute billions each year to environmental causes.

Patagonia, still privately held, continues to search out new ways to raise environmental consciousness. Whether you buy from them, sell to them, or compete with them, you are going to hear about the planetary crisis, and you will be asked to help.

In 1995, during a staff presentation, Chouinard said, "If you want to change government, change the corporations, and government will follow. If you want to change corporations, change consumers. Perhaps the real good that Patagonia could do was to use the company as a tool for social change, as a model to show other companies that a company can do well by taking the long view and doing the right thing."

In 1976, about the same time that Aveda and Patagonia were getting off the ground, four college buddies with a passion for statistics hung out their corporate shingle in the Research Triangle Park in Cary, North Carolina—Jim Goodnight, Tony Barr, John Sall, and Jane Hedwig were all founders of SAS Institute. (SAS stands for statistical analysis software, an application that reduces piles of raw data into manageable chunks of business intelligence.)

Initially, the company built software to analyze agricultural data, a college interest. But the founders quickly realized that many other industries, from banking to pharmaceuticals, could also benefit from their analysis software, so they drew up expansion plans, secured bank loans, and hired salespeople to call on companies. Barr managed the company's information systems, Sall oversaw a small group of programmers on various projects; and Hedwig focused on the software product documentation. Goodnight, eager to lead, took the role of CEO and president.

While other future high-tech titans designed distribution systems and graphical interfaces as their companies' foundation, Goodnight, who had a novel vision of how to design the perfect high-tech company, established a family-friendly employee life-style. SAS became a pioneer of the concept of work-life balance, especially for technology companies, which famously soaked eighty to one hundred hours a week from their employees.

Goodnight noticed that most software houses had employee programs that pulled families apart, wore away at worker health, and led to burnout. He knew he could do better. One of the first rules he implemented was a thirty-five-hour workweek: Overtime wasn't allowed, nor was working weekends.

Goodnight was a student of productivity and believed that most errors occur when an employee is working too much or too late. And he couldn't stomach putting his employees through the same hamster-on-a-treadmill work environment he'd witnessed when he'd visited a computer company while still in college. SAS also offered unlimited sick days; Goodnight knew that a sick employee on the job turned in poor work, made others ill, and took longer to mend.

A math whiz, Goodnight calculated that employee retention was a profit booster; he could tell you exactly what it would cost to replace lost programmers versus what it cost to give them free food, health care, fitness, and other services.

SAS Institute built its corporate campus based on Goodnight's vision. Like Patagonia, the company sponsored on-site day care for working parents. The corporate cafeteria served meals to employees as well as to their families and offered them high chairs and toys. In 1983, the company opened an on-site health care center staffed by family nurse practitioners, offering free services to any employee and his or her family; a state-of-the-art gymnasium soon followed.

On a typical workday, dozens of families eat lunch together, play on the corporate lawn, and swim in the company pool, making the campus resemble a resort more than a computer company. SAS has continually added new features for family, personal, and mental health, such as weekly deliveries of thousands of fresh flowers and an artist-in-residence program.

Even though, as a private company, SAS doesn't offer stock options, the turnover rate is less than 5 percent—about 70 percent lower than the industry average. The savings from reduced hiring and training costs adds up to more than $70 million per year. And the employees who stay are highly productive, bringing in an average of over half a million dollars in revenue per year.

Over the course of thirty years, SAS Institute has received continuous recognition. *Working Mother* magazine named it as one of the top employers for moms six years in a row. *Fortune* put it on the Best Companies to Work For list ten years in a row. In 2006, Oprah Winfrey named SAS the best company in America to work for.

The second wave of social innovation at SAS Institute rolled in with Goodnight's commitment to improve education in his company's backyard. He believes the best way to build a pipeline of future tech workers is to improve educational opportunities. He also believes he should reward the community that makes his business possible. Thus, in 1997, the company invested $15 million in a local, world-class college-prep school, the Cary Academy, and made it available to employees' families as well as community members.

SAS Institute, a major supporter of Communities In Schools, which helps troubled students graduate from school and pursue a college degree, also gives grants to local colleges and sponsors a leadership academy.

Like other pioneers, Goodnight is happy to share his insights with anyone who visits the SAS campus, and he has invited leading companies, from Google to IKEA, to send delegations to learn how to re-create the SAS experience.

These three innovators, from different industries and backgrounds, are united by motivation: mission as well as money. All three also decided not to take their companies public. In the early 1980s, because socially responsible investing was rare and stock market analysts scoffed at it, the pioneers chose to stay privately held, enjoying the freedom to work through the natural ups and downs of introducing a new value proposition. Chouinard told NBC News' Tom Brokaw, "I don't want some Wall Street greaseball running this company." Goodnight once told me that he'd "never report to a snot-nosed twentysomething analyst on Wall Street."

When the market for social value started to solidify in the 1990s, the pioneers were already generating profits through purpose, while changing the tastes of customers and employees one innovation at a time.

As the market for socially valuable business grows, pioneers are followed by another set of businesspeople: the fast followers.

Fast followers are innovators who, based on intelligence brought back from the front lines of their businesses, sense a values shift that will soon disrupt their current business model. They recognize the emergence of the new value proposition and act swiftly to place their companies ahead of the curve. Armed with a new business plan, they march into the future before the future marches into their backyard.

The difference between the pioneers and the fast followers goes beyond who comes first, however. It is also a matter of motivation. Both are driven by values, but the fast followers are driven by dollars as well. Pioneers want to change the world; fast followers want to win the game.

For example, take Jeffrey Immelt, CEO of General Electric. For many, the thought of General Electric being fast at anything defies logic; the company, with 300,000 employees, is enormous, turning out everything from jet engines and lightbulbs to hit television shows and credit cards.

Immelt took over the reins from former CEO Jack Welch on September 7, 2001, as the nation was in the throes of its first recession in ten years. His first years were tumultuous: Four days after his ascension came the terrorist attacks of September 11, and thereafter flowed a series of business shockers, from the collapses at Enron and WorldCom to a stock market that, after having loved the company for years, shrugged its shoulders, causing its stock to sag and infuriating investors accustomed to double-digit annual growth.

In 2004, with GE stock still moving sideways, Immelt huddled with his management team at the annual strategic planning session known to GEers as the "growth playbook meeting." Over the course of a few grueling days, managers made presentations and divulged questions that customers were asking about GE's greenhouse-gas emissions as well as its products' energy efficiency.

Beyond environmental concerns, several of GE's largest customers were also pushing for more energy savings from GE products in the future—or else. Meanwhile, Congress was considering legislation to limit companies' greenhouse-gas emissions, forcing them to pay a premium if they failed to comply.

GE was hardly an industry leader in the environmental field; most notoriously, it had polluted New York's Hudson River with PCBs, a by-product of its power-plant-transformer manufacturing, and had done little to clean it up while doing much to protest the cleanup requirements. The company was on track to have a 40 percent annual increase in greenhouse-gas emissions by 2012. Few of their key products led their category in energy efficiency ratings, and renewable energy was a back-burner issue in GE's research-and-development plans.

Immelt saw a storm coming. Realizing that a fast-growing segment of customers was asking for something entirely different from GE and its products, he told his team that these customer concerns were not bad news, just news: "We can use this to our advantage or be at the mercy of it."

Within a few months, Immelt approved a major business initiative, dubbed Ecomagination, through which the company promised to reduce, and eventually halt, the growth of its carbon footprint, and focus on building products that were "inherently green," met government standards, and reduced energy use by 10 percent or more than the product it would replace.

Immelt announced the project in May 2005. He gave his company five years to create a $20 billion business from clean technology, and committed 50 percent of GE's research-and-development budget to that goal—more than a billion dollars a year. The program also decreased GE's carbon emissions from a projected 40 percent increase by 2012 to a 1 percent drop, while continuing to grow the business.

Company managers soon were scrambling to beat competitors in energy efficiency in products ranging from jet engines to dishwashers. New products included water-treatment systems, solar roof tiles, and electric-fuel-cell-powered buses. The real estate division invested in green-building technology. All managers were asked to insert eco-friendliness into their strategy, much as they had been asked to insert quality into their strategy some twenty-five years previously. Reversing decades of stalling and stammering on GE's part, Immelt funded a 2009 plan to dredge the Hudson River of the pollutants and finally finish the required cleanup.

Like most fast followers, Immelt faced some serious struggles. He had to overcome a long-standing GE culture of putting profits first. Ecomagination required time and fiscal patience—a five-year plan at a time when Wall Street analysts, angry over a static stock price, were calling for a breakup of GE to reinvigorate its stock.

But Immelt's vision came to fruition faster than expected. GE sold more than $12 billion worth of eco-friendly products in 2006, including compact fluorescent lightbulbs, wind turbines, renewable energy products, and low-emissions engines—a 300 percent jump from 2004. Instead of increasing emissions as the company grew, they reduced them.

While Immelt doesn't forecast Ecomagination being a stock driver in the short or mid-term, GE is becoming more attractive to socially focused fund managers and their investors. Dozens of SRIs and sustainability indexes have added GE or purchased shares in the stock since 2005. Calvert Group senior vice president of research Bennett Freeman has said, "The effect of Ecomagination is huge. When GE commits to renewable energy, the argument is over in corporate America."

One of the world's biggest companies, Wal-Mart, is the next fast follower.

The thought of Wal-Mart as a fast follower in the Responsibility Revolution is more mind-boggling than conceiving of GE that way. Wal-Mart has long been known as an insular company. To do business with it required entering Wal-Mart World. Whether you were a city, a supplier, or an employee, everyone did things Wal-Mart's way. Its focus was profits and low prices rather than the general health of the world at large.

At least, that was Wal-Mart until 2004. CEO Lee Scott took over the company in late 2000 and promptly saw business sag—the stock declined more than 20 percent, even as protest groups such as Wal-Mart Watch wounded the company's reputation as Main Street America's best friend. A landmark class-action sexual discrimination suit unfolded in 2004, and a marketing executive was unceremoniously dismissed after she was accused of using Wal-Mart money to fund an internal affair.

In response, Wal-Mart went on a listening binge. Scott and a few dozen of his key executives logged more than a million miles of go-listen time, hearing from key suppliers, government officials, and even acrimonious watchdog groups, and conducting dozens of customer focus groups in order to grasp exactly what people thought of Wal-Mart.

They discovered what others already knew: The company was one of the biggest polluters on the planet. Its employees barely made a living wage; most could not afford health care insurance. The company's suppliers resented its practices. Hundreds of towns didn't want Wal-Mart to open stores there.

In vintage Wal-Mart style, Scott took, in his own words, "a defensive position on the matters." To him, fixing these problems was a cost driver, not a moneymaker.

Then, on August 23, 2005, Hurricane Katrina changed Scott's thinking. He visited wrecked stores and trashed communities. He spent time in Houston, meeting with victims living in the Astrodome—some of them Wal-Mart employees, others lifelong customers. The experience moved him.

Scott's team advised him that the best way to make Wal-Mart a better planetary citizen was by greening the business. Scott also realized that the programs that reduced carbon emissions, including energy efficiency and waste reduction, could save the retail giant millions of dollars, boosting its profitability in the long run.

Sixty days later, Scott gave a landmark speech to thousands of staffers titled "21st-Century Leadership." He admitted to a surprised audience that Wal-Mart had an image problem—and a need to address it. "These challenges . . . threaten all of us in the broader sense, but they also represent threats to the success of this business." He then laid out a plan to cut the company's carbon footprint, drive waste out of the supply chain, and convert to selling products that sustained the planet.

The first part of the program required Wal-Mart's fleet of more than 7,000 trucks to increase their fuel efficiency by 25 percent by the end of 2008. If Scott's goal is met, not only will Wal-Mart lower the amount of greenhouse gas added to the atmosphere, but it also will save $200 million per year.

The second part called for a store redesign to reduce energy use by 10 percent in three years and to install renewable energy wherever feasible. Scott approved a technology budget of $500 million for each of those years to reduce greenhouse gases produced by the stores. The company also agreed to share the technology it developed with anyone, including competitors such as Costco and Home Depot.

The program's third element was an initiative to slash solid waste by 20 percent by 2008, which led to a breakthrough in one of the most wasteful components of consumer products: packaging. Ninety percent of all the greenhouse gases that Wal-Mart emits are derived from its supply chain, and most of that from packaging.

Scott realized that requiring Wal-Mart's 60,000-plus suppliers to reduce dramatically the size of product packaging would save store space, decrease transportation costs, and lessen the amount of waste the company released into the environment. The plan calls for reusing or recycling 100 percent of the packaging flowing through Wal-Mart's entire supply chain and stores by 2025.

Next, Scott created an initiative to put organic products on store shelves. Traditionally grown cotton and food fosters pesticide use and groundwater pollution. Scott commanded his buyers to start the shift to organic.

Finally, corporate buyers were challenged to source most foods either regionally or locally. As one of Wal-Mart's produce department executives, Ron McCormick, described it, the question was: "How can we reduce food miles?"

Scott's plans were immediately met with skepticism—groups from the Sierra Club to Wal-Mart Watch called it "greenwashing," an eco-based publicity stunt. However, one environmentalist, Ashok Gupta of the Natural Resource Defense Council, did say this: "It seems that Wal-Mart's serious. And if they even do half of what they say they're going to do, it's going to make a huge difference for the planet."

Fast-forward to May 2006: John Fleming, the chief marketing officer for Wal-Mart, announced the successful implementation of multiple organic food lines and promised that they would be priced only 10 percent higher than conventional foods. Wal-Mart was now selling more organic milk than any other store in the country. By the end of 2008, it will pass Whole Foods and Wild Oats combined in selling organic foods.

Under the watchful eye of the media, Wal-Mart innovated, scrimped, and shaved energy use from its business operations. In July 2007, the company reported that its truck fleet had achieved a 15 percent jump in fuel efficiency. But the biggest story at Wal-Mart concerns a single product: the lightbulb.

When Wal-Mart execs met with Steve Hamburg, an environmental studies professor at Brown University, Scott boasted about Wal-Mart's plans; Hamburg told them that they were still missing the biggest opportunity to change the world. In his view, Wal-Mart should focus on changing its customers' home-lighting strategies.

Hamburg explained that half of all greenhouse-gas emissions in the world come from power plants, and that half of all power plants exist to keep the lights on.

At the time, about 97 percent of domestic lightbulbs were incandescent. Yet the swirl-shaped compact fluorescent lightbulb, or the CFL, is 75 percent more efficient than an incandescent lightbulb, and it lasts ten to twenty times longer.

Here's how Wal-Mart figured Hamburg's suggestion would yield savings: If 100 million Wal-Mart customers replaced just one traditional lightbulb with a CFL, the daily energy savings could provide a day's worth of electricity for a city of 1.5 million people. Using two bulbs would be the emissions-reduction equivalent of 1.3 million fewer cars on the road every day.

And, thought Wal-Mart, if these customers saved $30 over the life of the lightbulb, they would give that money back to Wal-Mart by buying lawn chairs, fencing, and other products.

In October 2006, Wal-Mart held a "Lightbulb Summit" in Las Vegas for suppliers and vendors, with environmentalists and government officials as speakers. Wal-Mart also staged a two-day session to educate attendees about their CFL plan.

After the summit, a GE executive told his Wal-Mart contact, "Don't go too fast, guys. We have all these plants that produce traditional bulbs. What are we going to do about those?" Wal-Mart's reply: "We're going there. It's up to you to decide if you're coming with us."

A few months later, Scott and GE's Immelt hammered out a partnership: GE ramped up CFL production and Osram Sylvania did the same. Jim Jubb, Sylvania's vice president of consumer products, told *Fast Company* magazine, "When Wal-Mart sets their mind to something this specific and this narrow, believe me, they're going to get their way."

Wal-Mart did get its way. It used its merchandising prowess to showcase the swirl bulb. In the past, a compact fluorescent lightbulb sat on the bottom shelf, causing buyers to bend over and squint to see exactly what this funny-shaped bulb was, if they noticed it at all. Now store managers moved the CFLs up into prime eye-level real estate. They also used the swirl-shaped bulbs in all the light fixtures they sold, creating interest among shoppers. Finally, they gave up precious space at the end of store aisles to post signs educating customers on how much money they would save if they made the switch. By the summer of 2007, Wal-Mart had sold almost 50 million CFLs.

These fast followers illustrate Harvard professor Henry Chesbrough's definition of the word *innovation*: when invention is successfully brought to market. Not only did these companies succeed in bringing their unconventional ideas to life, they did so despite being both publicly held and huge.

The risks were considerable. GE has often won *Fortune*'s Most Admired Company in America award, and for the last twenty years, Wal-Mart has sold more products than any other company in the world. So when you see companies that are among America's most admired and feared embracing the same change, what do you have? A revolution that is too legit to quit.

Fast followers help to legitimize the pioneers who preceded them. Muddled managers at most companies might have rolled their eyes when they heard about Goodnight's employee perks in North Carolina, but they must have been startled when they heard that tech powerhouse Google, another fast follower, was not only acting similarly by offering employee perks such as free gourmet meals, massages, on-site dental and health care, and a world-class gym, but making a handsome profit as well.

Other highly successful companies emerged as fast followers during this period, including Starbucks (fair-trade coffee), Toyota (hybrid cars), Citigroup Inc. (community development), and British Petroleum (renewable energy). As of the end of 2007, fast followers can be found within almost all major industries.

Innovators introduce the new value proposition to the masses. In the Quality Revolution, fast movers such as Japan's Ricoh, Motorola, and Florida Power & Light gave millions of Americans a sample of high-quality electronics, office supplies, and customer service, forever changing their tastes.

Today's fast followers have acted similarly to move the Responsibility Revolution to the threshold of the disruptive phase. Together with the pioneers, they've introduced a new value proposition: Contribute to the greater good with your money or your talent.

Once the growing flock of ThemGeners gets a taste of purpose with a paycheck, there's no going back. They'll expect it everywhere, in every industry, throughout all walks of life.

When the market becomes infected with a new value proposition, the innovation phase is complete. What follows next will be a bumpy ride for some and an ugly crash for many: Welcome to the scary part of the revolution—the disruptive phase.

6

Phase Four: Disruption

T he end of the last Ice Age, which occurred between 9,000 and 13,000 years ago, was a highly disruptive time for the woolly mammoth. Long adapted to the cold, this mega-mammal flourished in a frozen environment. But as the ice sheets started cracking and then retreating, life for mammoths got ugly. They lost their food sources (a by-product of the changing climate), their reproduction rate decreased, and their numbers shrank.

To make matters worse, they were losing their habitat to the mammalian revolutionaries of the times: the humans who were crossing the Bering Strait from Asia to North America. No match for their new predators, the mammoths, living in the wrong place at the wrong time, disappeared forever.

Unlike in the Ice Age, in today's Information Age, survival is a choice rather than a destiny. The just-for-profit mammoths of the world have the ability to recognize cracks in their economic ice, a fast-changing business climate, and the arrival of revolutionary predators. They can embrace the changes, adapt, and thrive—if they can see the signs and make the moves.

The disruptive phase is a period during which companies that don't adhere to the new values suffer losses in critical business areas.

Disruption generally begins in the industries where the new value is most lacking. Eventually, it spills over into every industry. This phase is often marked by incumbent industry leaders being toppled or, at the least, highly diminished by market pressures.

The disruptive phase of the Responsibility Revolution will cause tens of thousands of American businesses to suffer great losses, forcing them either to adapt or to shrivel. They will lose customers, talent, and capital. And, especially for those companies whose leaders live in a state of denial, interlopers will chip away at their remaining profitability until finally they can no longer survive.

Those companies that do survive the disruptive phase of the Responsibility Revolution—I call them the late followers—will experience tremendous upheaval.

The laggards will dig in their heels, deny there are cracks in the ice, and foolishly try to wrestle with the revolutionaries. They face the same future as the mammoth.

The disruptive phase of this revolution is already under way.

Consider the computer company Dell. Five years ago, it was standing on cracking ice. Dell had a choice to make: follow the new values or suffer painful losses.

The cracking started in March 2002 with the release of a tongue-in-cheek report titled "Dude, Why Won't They Take Back My Computer?," prepared by the Computer TakeBack Campaign, a coalition of two dozen activist groups focused on the responsible disposal of computers. The report revealed that Dell didn't offer American consumers the ability to recycle old computers, resulting in millions ending up in landfills every year.

Computers, especially monitors, contain dangerous toxins such as lead and mercury that will eventually find their way from the landfill to the groundwater supply. This report highlighted what the EPA had been saying for years—that electronic waste was the fastest-growing form of trash in the world. Widely read, the report bruised Dell's otherwise sterling reputation for social responsibility.

One month later, the Texas Campaign for the Environment, a member of the Computer TakeBack Campaign, issued a press release revealing that Dell offered a program in Europe where, for a fee, consumers could have their old Dell computers properly recycled.

Dell provided this service because it was the law in Europe. However, in the United States, where no laws mandated computer disposal, the service wasn't available. The executive director for the Texas Campaign for the Environment, Robin Schneider, posed the question "Why do American consumers and the American environment deserve second-class treatment?" This generated national media attention and pulled an important organization into the fray: the Calvert Group.

The Calvert Group, an SRI firm, held a significant position in Dell and wanted an immediate about-face in the company's recycling policy. Thus, in May 2002, Calvert announced its intention to file, at Dell's annual meeting, a shareholder resolution requiring it to conduct a study to identify its liabilities and risks from electronic waste, and then implement a plan to address them.

Shareholder resolutions are highly disruptive to annual meetings because they take the focus off future products and revenue. In 2002, Dell's stock price was reeling from the burst of the dotcom bubble, the Enron scandal, and the terrorist attacks of September 11, 2001. The company wanted anything but a debate about how much lead or mercury was in a dead Dell.

Calvert had considerable weight to throw around. According to the *Austin Business Journal*, it owned 17.7 percent of Dell's outstanding shares—at the time, more than the 12 percent that Dell CEO Michael Dell himself owned.

So when Calvert talked, Dell listened. After a frantic set of phone calls, Dell agreed to begin the liability study and roll out a limited program to take back computers. Calvert then withdrew the resolution. But the TakeBack Campaign was dissatisfied with the out-of-meeting settlement, feeling that Dell's promised program failed to address the real problems with its products—and charged consumers too much for recycling. Additionally, to save money, Dell's recycling vendor, UNICOR, employed prison inmates to dismantle equipment (exempt from traditional occupational safety laws). Pulling apart computer electronics is far more dangerous for inmates than breaking rocks in the hot sun.

In July, dozens of members of the Computer TakeBack Campaign showed up at Dell's annual meeting. Outside, they held picket signs and shouted into bullhorns. Inside, taking advantage of a provision that allows any shareholder to submit questions for executives to answer, activists put Michael Dell through a grueling set of questions, and the meeting broke down into arguments and catcalls.

Still, Dell continued with its plans and hired a public relations firm to help mend its environmental reputation with a nine-city tour, during which staffers picked up computers for recycling—but without telling consumers that they would be dismantled by conscripted prison labor. In full combat mode, according to Schneider, "We threw everything we had at them in 2003."

In January 2003, the Computer TakeBack Campaign released its annual Computer Report Card at the Consumer Electronics Show in Las Vegas. The Report Card measures the environmental performance of thirty computer makers. Dell not only received a failing grade, but also received a dishonorable mention because it used prison labor.

Bad timing for Dell—Michael Dell was making his first keynote appearance at the conference. And it didn't help that activists dressed as old-fashioned jailbirds protested there, posing for pictures in front of Dell's trade-show booth. Local and national newspapers ran pictures of the striped demonstrators repeatedly over the next few months.

By May 2003, Dell had had its first sit-down meeting with managers from the Calvert Group, who had joined the TakeBack Campaign in their support for safe working conditions for recyclers. During the same month, the TakeBack Campaign targeted one of Dell's major shareholders: Susan Dell, Michael's wife. A dress designer with a store in a tony Austin, Texas, neighborhood, she was showing off her new line at the shop. Protesters decided to stage their own fashion show, so they gathered up some electronic waste, a glue gun, and some secondhand clothes. After putting together a motley line of e-waste fashion, they paraded down a makeshift runway in front of Susan's store and handed out pamphlets educating people on the hazards of e-waste. The local fashion media picked up the story and ran a favorable review of the protesters' sense of style rather than one of Ms. Dell's.

The gambits paid off. In July 2003, Dell announced that it would change recycling vendors to ensure occupational-safety compliance. Furthermore, Dell promised to take back any consumer's old computer, regardless of make. Pat Nathan, Dell's executive in charge of sustainability, publicly thanked the market campaign and the Calvert Group for their influence in getting Dell to "come around and become an advocate for social responsibility in recycling."

According to the TakeBack Campaign's Schneider, "Getting an industry leader like that to change its policy in eighteen months is really quick." Dell, which responded to intensely disruptive market pressures to protect its reputation with consumers, is a survival story.

Meanwhile, in Detroit, the ice was cracking all around the Big Three automakers as their market share in the United States retreated precipitously. The Prius, Toyota's hybrid car, was becoming the *it* car for socially conscious drivers: movie stars Leonardo DiCaprio and Cameron Diaz drove theirs to the 2003 Oscars, while actor Larry David bought two for himself and one to drive on his popular sitcom, *Curb Your Enthusiasm*. In 2004, both *Car and Driver* and *Motor Trend* magazines named the Prius Car of the Year.

At the same time that Toyota was speeding past Detroit into the green future, it was laying down American roots by opening more factories, creating jobs, and supporting the local communities in which it operated.

For example, in San Antonio, Texas, the site of its newest factory, Toyota launched a literacy campaign for anyone who couldn't read or write in English; it also dispatched its top quality gurus to help local hospitals improve their operations. From Iowa to Alabama, the company became involved in numerous community activities, especially by sponsoring dozens of local Little League teams.

All these investments paid off for Toyota's reputation, helping the company gain market share in the South and the Midwest, where "buy American" was still the prevailing mind-set. In 2005 and 2006, *Fortune* named Toyota America's Most Admired Car Company—despite its being based in Japan.

At the same time, Toyota was helping to position its rival American cars as gas-guzzling technology laggards. The only American hybrid available was Ford's Escape, which was powered by Toyota's hybrid technology, and it didn't catch on. As the price of gas sky-rocketed and global warming concerns rose, so did Toyota's earn-ings and market share. Everything took off, including sales of its high-quality nonhybrids, such as the Camry, as well as the Tundra, its new truck.

Why? Americans thought that Toyota had a lock on miles per gal-lon. In June 2006, GM's chief market strategist, Paul Ballew, told Wall Street analysts that "Detroit automakers weren't getting full credit for their fuel economy scores. You look at the manufacturer that has added the most large-truck capacity here in the last few years—it happens to be Toyota. But they are getting credit because they sell a whopping 100,000 Priuses." What he didn't say, or under-stand, is that the GM brand had become stodgy and old-fashioned in the minds of Americans.

In 2007, *BusinessWeek* and research firm Interbrand conducted a study to assess the most valuable global brands. Toyota emerged as the most valuable auto brand and the sixth most valuable interna-tional brand—a 15 percent increase in brand equity in just one year. According to Interbrand, the reason for this was that the Prius had "a halo effect on the Toyota range as a whole." In other words, Amer-ican consumers saw all Toyotas as lean and green machines.

By summer of 2007, for the first time in history, Detroit had lost its market share lead in the United States. Collectively, the Big Three held only a 48 percent market share. And just one year later, Toyota leapfrogged Ford to become the number two car company domesti-cally, second only to GM. GM, Ford, and DaimlerChrysler put hy-brids and fuel-cell cars at the top of their agenda and poured hundreds of millions of dollars into clawing their way back into favor, laying off workers and scaling back benefits to compensate.

The last time Detroit suffered losses this deep was during the

Quality Revolution in the mid-1980s, when its domestic market share dropped by 10 percent in less than two years. Whom did they lose to last time? The Japanese, led by Toyota. Now they were losing share to them again, even as Toyota endured a record number of recalls.

Why did this lapse in quality fail to damage Toyota's reputation? Because the public was looking for something new in a car: social value. In the words of baseball philosopher Yogi Berra, "It's déjà vu all over again."

While these stories are currently confined to a small group of industry leaders, they illustrate the future of thousands of companies that lack either a good social reputation or a strong social value proposition.

Unless a company is an innovator for good, business conditions will get ugly. This is due mostly to three emerging market conditions that will create disruptive clashes over scarce business resources. As these three market shifts play out, they will find their way into every crack and crevice of business life as we know it.

1. The End of the Casual Customer

Mindful customers are the enemy of the thoughtless business. They don't buy based only on price or quality. They ask too many questions about the product: how it was made, where it comes from, who helped make it. And they tell their friends where and what to buy— and those friends listen.

With each passing year, Americans' purchasing values are being reshaped by the context of modern life. Two separate forces are driving this change—and again, it all comes back to demographic trends.

The Boomer Generation is massive enough to disrupt the talent pool upon its members' retirement. What do retirees do with their newfound spare time? They shop, they judge, and they talk to their friends and family.

The only group comparable in size to the boomers is today's youth. They also shop, judge, and talk. Put those two groups together and you have an army for good. How big an army? More than half of the American population by 2020.

Researcher Andrew Zolli outlined how this scenario will play out in a 2006 article in *Fast Company* magazine: "Over the next twenty years, this group is going to grow explosively as American society becomes a demographic 'hourglass,' with the largest populations of old and young people in its history living together. The psychological principle at play is that the older you get, the more you think about the planet you're leaving behind, and conversely, the younger you are, the more you cling to your idealism."

The second driver of the conscious marketplace will be the education of what I call the casual consumer, the group of more than 100 million Americans who at this point in time shop mostly for price, features, or quality, and seldom read labels for anything beyond nutritional value.

Typically, this group is unwilling to pay more, or accept less, for socially responsible products or services. They aren't aware of available substitutes for many of the products or companies that they know in their heart aren't socially good.

They are primed, though. Researchers say even these casual consumers are developing strong feelings about workers' rights, justice, and the planetary crisis.

Several educational forces will change the way they buy. For example, Wal-Mart is in full-teach mode, devoting valuable store space to displays that educate millions of daily shoppers about the benefits of organic food and clothing, energy-efficient products, and fair-trade coffees and teas. Store managers are being trained to answer questions and advise first-time buyers in these categories.

Then there is the education that comes from buying, using, and enjoying these new products. Ted Ning, executive editor of the *LOHAS Journal*, told me that "Wal-Mart is providing goods that were typically available to an upscale and largely Caucasian demographic to the masses for the first time. Organic food, cotton, fair-trade shrimp, CFL bulbs, all of these will be on sale, at low prices, at Wal-Mart."

For price-driven shoppers, social quality is about to become affordable. Wal-Mart's size will contribute to the scale necessary for these products' prices to drop dramatically. What's more, according to Ning, "this will influence all of its customers' buying behavior, causing them to look for green or organic in the purchases they make everywhere."

Several decades ago, health information on labels heightened awareness of sugar, fat, and later trans fats, driving a paradigm shift in shopping. Today, in the United Kingdom, where ethical consumerism is enormously popular, companies are putting environmental and other social metrics on labels next to health information. Labels on soda bottles, for example, report how many pounds of carbon were released into the atmosphere to produce them.

This labeling program was created by the Carbon Trust, which includes big brands such as PepsiCo, Cadbury Schweppes, and Marks & Spencer. It's expected to spread to the United States by early 2009 and to become mainstream a few years later.

LEK Consulting, a UK firm that helps big brands with marketing projects, conducted a 2007 study to measure the impact of these new labels on consumers, finding that "close to half of consumers would change their buying behavior in some way and an equal number would switch to a product or service with a lower carbon footprint, even if it was not their first preference."

So what happens if SUVs become the mink coats of our generation, as may well happen given the rise in the cost of gasoline? Almost 90 percent of Detroit's profits stem from SUVs. If a sudden and significant drop in demand for SUVs occurred, tens of thousands of workers would lose their jobs. What is going to happen to bottled water, or electronics containing lead or mercury? We will soon find out.

Companies that become socially unpopular will lose in brand strength, and brand is worth at least 20 percent of a large company's value. As low price, high quality, and high status yield to fair, green, and helpful, the brand landscape will change. The most common customer inquiry will shift from "What will it cost me?" to "What will this cost everyone?"

2. The End of the Deep Talent Pool

In the past, when talent was abundant and outsourcing promised to fill any labor gap, losing a qualified candidate was an inconvenience. ExxonMobil losing an engineer to British Petroleum meant hiring one of many other candidates standing in line; Kroger's losing a store manager to Kmart meant replacing that person with another in a sea of applicants.

About the time that *BusinessWeek* and Net Impact were conducting their study on the rise of social career values, other researchers were looking into a related labor issue. In 1998, McKinsey & Company released a report, *The War for Talent*, which suggested that the most critical resource in the 2010s would be talent—and that talent would be in short supply.

In the report, lead consultant Charles Fishman explained the coming demographic trends: "In fifteen years, there will be 15 percent fewer Americans in the 35- to 45-year-old range than there are now. At the same time, the U.S. economy is likely to grow at a rate of 3 percent to 4 percent per year. So over that period, the demand for bright, talented 35- to 45-year-olds will increase by, say, 25 percent, and the supply will be going down by 15 percent. That sets the stage for a talent war."

In 2004, several reports confirmed the coming talent shortage, including Deloitte Research, which identified 2008 as the year the first wave of baby boomers would begin to retire, with three out of four hiring managers expecting a talent shortfall starting within a few years.

The signs of talent shortages are already visible. According to the National Science Foundation, industry demand in the pharmaceuticals business for scientists now outstrips supply by a margin of three to one; the technology industry faces the same crisis because of a shortage of highly skilled engineers. Given that most companies' value is dependent on the talent needed to execute business plans and manage the workforce, economists generally place talent's value at approximately 50 percent of a company's worth.

The war for talent will not be won with money. ThemGeners are willing to take a pay cut to work for a company they'd be proud to post as their employer on their Facebook or LinkedIn profile page. Increasingly, the battle for talent comes down to reputation rather than compensation.

After talking with more than five hundred HR execs, researchers at *Human Resources* magazine learned that the reputation of a company, its culture, and the work environment were at the top of the list as talent attractors, especially of skilled and managerial employees.

Where did the paycheck and benefits land in this list? Last.

Some companies will respond by juicing up pay packages or broadening their advertising programs; these tactics may bring some talent in the door, but at the same time, the added expenses will hit the bottom line, taking money away from critical business functions such as product development and marketing.

At the same time as the talent pool shrinks, the body of information available to talent expands. The workers of the future are likely to have more information about your company than your company can gather about them.

I've sat in on several recruiting roundtables connected to my work with Yahoo! Hot Jobs, a popular job board. Over and over, recruiters point out how much time highly qualified candidates spend Googling their potential employers to find out everything they can before making a decision. What are they searching for? A progressive company that has both feet in the twenty-first century.

In the future, job seekers will turn down offers from companies that fail the do-they-get-it? test. In the view of ThemGeners, a company gets it if it integrates social values into every part of the business. If a company has a glaring social deficiency, its good points will not be enough to attract top talent. In other words, if a company such as Wal-Mart has a green strategy but doesn't give their workers a living wage or health care coverage, it doesn't get it.

One issue that will separate companies that get it from those that don't will be inclusiveness. Companies are inclusive if they offer equal opportunities and benefits to workers regardless of race, religious beliefs, gender, or sexual orientation.

I recently had a chance to talk with a recruiter from the industrial supplies manufacturer Honeywell Corporation. During a job interview in 2007, an engineering candidate asked him, "Does the company offer same-sex dependent coverage?"

The recruiter then asked, "Why, are you gay?"

The candidate replied, "No, I'm evolved. I want to make sure I work for a company that is, too."

Companies that overlook this issue will be cast as outdated by ThemGeners, and the longer they wait to make the leap, the less credibility they will have when they do. This is the nature of business revolutions.

3. The End of the Nearsighted Investor

The biggest polluters and worst employers have generally found traditional investors easy to do business with. They share the same time horizon—ninety days—and if these investors make a profit, they ask few questions. In their view, a business's responsibility to society is to make money, and lots of it.

This cozy arrangement is ending. As mentioned, one out of eight investment dollars is currently screened for social profits and losses. As with talent and customers, that's not enough to change the rules of investing—yet. At some point in the next ten years, a critical mass of farsighted investors will put the squeeze on just-for-profit companies and redistribute the juice to top corporate citizens.

This paradigm shift will be the result of two disruptive trends: social investing going mainstream, and mainstream investing going social.

Up until now, despite the explosive growth of SRI funds, a low percentage of Americans have had a chance to invest according to their values. To do so, they'd have to buy a mutual fund or certain individual stocks. That requires disposable income.

The Wal-Mart of personal investing is the retirement-fund industry—and this is where Middle America's investment dollars live. Retirement assets are the third-largest piece of the market, trailing only banks and mutual funds.

Of those assets, more than half lie in defined-contribution accounts such as 401(k)s; the other half are administered in defined-benefit accounts such as union pension plans.

The fastest-growing segment of retirement plans is direct contribution, in which the individual investors select their risk tolerance as well as specific funds in which to invest. Up until recently, only one in five plans offered SRI funds among their options.

That number is about to triple. According to a July 2007 study released by Mercer Investment Consulting, 41 percent of plan sponsors will be adding SRIs to their options within three years, bringing the total penetration to six out of ten plans by 2010. The authors say that the main forces behind this trend include a desire to align retirement-plan offerings with the mission of the employer (e.g., a focus on corporate social responsibility), internal staff recommendations, and employee/participant requests for SRI options.

Will conservative investors in Iowa select an SRI retirement plan over the S&P 500? According to more than 81 percent of plan administrators, many will—some driven by environmental fears, others motivated by media coverage of innovators and their accomplishments. And those who don't choose an SRI initially will start to think about doing so.

A few weeks after this study was released, Calvert Group CEO Barbara Krumsiek wrote, "We are indeed at the tipping point in a redefinition of mainstream investing. The growth in assets under SRI management and the explosive growth in the availability of SRI funds to investors, particularly in the 401(k) retirement programs, bode well for continued growth in the coming 15 years."

Much as Wal-Mart's store shelves educate the masses about pesticides or greenhouse gases, retirement funds are about to expose tens of millions of people to a way of creating financial security. The masses are getting new investment glasses.

Meanwhile, there's a new yardstick of success that the mainstream market will be using to value companies: the triple bottom line. Coined by British environmentalist John Elkington, this accounting method still considers profits, but also takes into account a company's positive, as well as negative, impact on workers, communities, and the environment. This perspective helps investors looking at the company avoid missing its future liabilities or assets.

Several recent events have helped publicize this new formula. In 2006, the United Nations launched the Principles for Responsible Investment (PRI), a code of ethics for mainstream investors. Twenty prominent leaders from twelve countries in the institutional investment industry developed the principles and canvassed the global stock market for signatories.

According to the UN's PRI Report on Progress 2007 study, by the end of July 2007 more than two hundred international investment firms and fund managers—with a total of $9 trillion under management—have voluntarily agreed to abide by the UN Principles for Responsible Investment. According to most experts, this number could double before the end of fiscal year 2010.

Mainstream investors who are not swept up by the momentum of socially responsible thinking may be converted to triple-bottom-line thinking by the statistics. According to a 2007 study conducted by senior researchers at Goldman Sachs, "Companies that are considered leaders in environmental, social and governance (ESG) policies are also leading the pack in stock performance—by an average of 25 percent since 2005."

The study also revealed that in seven out of ten cases, companies with great ESG performance crushed their just-for-profit competitors over the same period, as measured by profits or market share.

Future developments will also drive the mainstream's move to assessing the triple bottom line. The global warming crisis will fan its flames as a rush of companies join GE in making profits with clean technologies. These companies will be rewarded by investors with rich valuations, just like early-stage Internet players.

In addition, many companies will likely be sideswiped by quickly changing regulatory conditions. Within a few years, it's likely that states, or even the federal government, will ratify corporate carbon emissions taxes, mandate minimum health care coverage for workers, and/or require fair-trade disclosure on product packaging. Any one of these changes could add new expenses or hurdles for incumbent industry leaders, scaring off nervous investors and causing fund managers to reevaluate some of the blue-chip stocks they've been touting for years.

The number of shareholder resolutions calling for companies to analyze their triple bottom line, and report it openly, has increased by 500 percent since 2002. Most analysts believe that the SEC will make this type of reporting mandatory for public companies within the next decade. The result will be a social transparency that reveals the warts as well as the pearls in a company's operations.

You would think that most smart business leaders would see the signs of impending disruption to their business models and respond immediately. Remarkably, few do.

Some react by denial. For example, at Dell Computer's 2002 annual shareholders' meeting, CEO Michael Dell insisted that there was no consumer demand for computer recycling in the United States. Executives at Safeway scoffed at Whole Foods' decision to stop selling live lobsters because it was cruel. Oracle's Larry Ellison cracked jokes about the excessive employee perks at Google. The more leaders remain in denial, the more disconnected their companies become from the market environment.

These leaders, whose only option is a cram course as shareholders, debtors, and employees clamor for change, will have to play catch-up under the watchful eyes of analysts and investors—making everyone's work stressful and arduous. Meanwhile, they are exposing their employees to dislocation, such as companywide layoffs and pay cuts due to a loss in market share, profitability, or stock price.

When a company lags behind market forces, everyone within it is culpable. Too many middle managers and other able-minded professionals refuse to step up to generate the right response at the right time. Like their CEOs, most of the rank and file want to believe what's happening is all just a phase or a fad. It isn't.

7

Phase Five: The New Order

The establishment of the New Order takes place when the new value becomes a source of competitive advantage for all.

Social responsibility will be the new king. Companies that contribute more than they deduct from people, community, and planet will make more money and will be more attractive as business partners.

Much of the New Order phase of the Responsibility Revolution lies in the future—as does its description—but there is one industry where the New Order is already manifest: the $10 billion carpet-manufacturing industry.

The carpet industry went through the disruptive phase in the mid-1990s. Today, surprisingly, generating net social value is a top priority—surprising because, socially speaking, carpet manufacturing can be one of the world's nastiest industries.

Carpet is made largely of petroleum-based products such as nylon and contains two key carcinogenic ingredients—fiberglass and polyvinyl chloride (PVC). Until 1997, almost 98 percent of all carpet ended up in landfills, where it would take 50,000 years to break down. Most companies or residences use carpet for only eight years before discarding it. At the time, carpet comprised almost 2 percent of all solid waste in the world.

The disruptive phase in that industry was led by Interface's Ray Anderson, as discussed in the introduction to this book.

Interface began offering products that satisfied its newly environmentally-aware customers and irrevocably changed the rules of the carpet business. And Interface profited from these changes—by 1999, it had doubled its market share, saving more than $300 million as a by-product of its waste-reduction program.

Interface's key competitors, including Shaw Carpet, Milliken, and Mohawk Carpet, saw the writing on the wall and started to retool their businesses to offer sustainable carpet solutions as well. They hired consultants and leading environmentalists, aggressively moving to realign themselves with the shifting market.

In 1999, taking a cue from Interface, Shaw Carpet launched its nonpolyvinyl carpet backing and the next year purchased a reclaiming company to recycle used carpet. Two years later, Mohawk released a type of carpet made entirely of recycled plastic bottles, reducing their reliance on more-dangerous and scarce virgin petroleum products.

Then, in 2002, every major producer of carpet—including their core chemical suppliers, BASF, DuPont, and Honeywell—signed the National Carpeting Recycling Agreement, creating an industrywide organization to recover and recycle used carpet.

Today, the carpet industry is the only one in America that complies with the International Kyoto Protocol by emitting fewer carbon emissions than it did in 1990, even though it is producing 40 percent more carpet.

The carpet industry's new social order reached beyond environmental issues. Once Interface got the industry's attention by reducing its environmental impact, it began focusing on making social contributions by improving the quality of life for its workers, thus attracting talent and improving productivity.

Joyce LaValle, who had been promoted several times since she gave CEO Ray Anderson a copy of *The Ecology of Commerce*, was appointed to run human resources for Interface in 1999 and was asked to help align the worker experience with the company's new vision. Now that the company was acting sustainably with the planet, it was time for it to act as compassionately with its own employees.

In 1997, LaValle was given the job of turning around Bently Prince Street, a company Interface had recently acquired, where morale and productivity were low. Among LaValle's many initiatives was the launch of a new line of carpet called Women at Work, whose marketing materials and product packaging featured photos of female workers at the plant.

Her efforts produced immediate results: Productivity jumped and word got out that Prince Street was a good place to work. Within a few years, LaValle launched companywide programs, including call centers for health and safety and same-sex dependent health care coverage—the first such policy for an industry located in one of the most conservative areas in the country.

By 2000, applications for jobs at Interface far exceeded openings and the company's excellent reputation became a competitive source of advantage, causing Milliken, Mohawk, and Shaw Carpet to change how they, too, approached other areas of the business besides the environment. Today, employee recognition and inclusion are must-have elements in any industry leader's HR programs.

As the Responsibility Revolution unfolds, five rules of the New Order will become clear:

1. The longer it takes to join the Responsibility Revolution, the more expensive it will be to realign in order to catch up with the innovators.

It won't be sufficient for a company simply to announce its changes; the company will have to convince everyone that its intentions are sincere, and this effort will require major efforts in marketing and public relations.

In the early 1990s, when Ford finally decided to embrace quality, it had to invest many millions in a long-term "Quality Is Job One" campaign to attempt to achieve credibility in the eyes of the media and car buyers.

2. Integration is as important as innovation in the long term.

Radical breakthrough inventions won't reimagine an industry; what will is the injection of new values into all parts of the business, from product to partner to people. Companies that fail to integrate fully will have gaping holes in their business model compared with those that allow the new mission to guide all their operations.

3. Progress must be measured and reported.

These metrics will measure a company's diverse social values, including employee quality of life, ethics in the supply chain, and its impacts on host communities and on the larger natural environment. Much like financial accounting, social accounting will include a plus side and a minus side (contribution to versus damage done to society), making it easy to assess a company's net social value alongside its net financial value.

4. Companies must provide rewards for adding social value.

The most effective way to get everyone on board is to reward as many employees as necessary for helping the company meet the newly established metrics. Rewards can take the form of compensation bonuses, promotions, or some creative form of recognition.

5. Companies must stay focused on the new value.

Many innovator companies paving the way for a revolution eventually fall victim to it because they don't stick to their original commitments.

For example, in order to make its numbers and expand its product line to meet the stock market's expectations, personal-care products retailer The Body Shop made the leap from private to public; in doing so, the company licensed technology from companies that conducted animal testing—in direct violation of the company's original mission. Exposed by the media, The Body Shop saw its stock swoon and its sales drop. To this day, the brand has not recovered its stature.

A final note about the New Order—for many of you it will bring welcome news. Here's why: You may already be practicing socially responsible behavior at home. You recycle trash, think about fuel emissions, volunteer to help gather toys for tots at Christmas, or shop at the local farmers' market and buy from local merchants.

Maybe you've been frustrated that you've had to leave those sensibilities at home; by the time you arrive at your job, you're no longer someone who thinks about good, but someone who thinks only about work. Maybe you've reluctantly swallowed your conscience from nine to five.

One of the greatest blessings of the Responsibility Revolution is that you'll be able to take your values to work with you instead of leaving them at home. In fact, your company desperately needs you to do so.

The Responsibility Revolution's unique offer is this: the chance to lead a purpose-driven life, 24/7/365.

———

A good hard rain is a-gonna fall on the business landscape. This rain is necessary, and it will transform the world at work as we know it.

I've painted a picture full of dark clouds, complete with lightning strikes that move closer and closer as time goes by. This rain will not be soft. It will move from disruptive droplets to torrential downpours, wiping out business rules and customs that have been in operation for decades. Whatever is not fully rooted on higher ground will be washed away.

When this cleansing rain finally subsides, a lot of familiar names will no longer be corporate leaders; they may well be joining that rusted heap of has-beens such as Braniff Airlines, Commodore Computers, Woolworth's, and Oldsmobile, all of whom failed to change with the times.

These changes aren't going away. No one's going to make an announcement in two years that fair trade isn't required because the developing world no longer needs justice. No one's going to say that global warming's been reversed due to lack of interest. The issues will only become greater over time.

These new values won't be limited to just the business world, either. Your children will study them in school during civics and economics lessons. Business students will take courses in corporate social responsibility, sustainability, ethics, and community development; they are already required at places such as Northwestern's Kellogg School and Columbia Business School.

Social values are also taking root in churches, led by Senior Pastor Joel Hunter at Longwood Florida's Northland Church. In 2006, Hunter and ninety other pastors, including Rick Warren (author of *The Purpose Driven Life*), signed the Evangelical Climate Initiative, which claims that global warming is a sinful crisis that all God's children have a moral duty to correct. Throughout the nation, pastors have begun to preach the "Green Gospel," and innumerable churches have begun sustainability programs; similar movements are occurring in Catholicism and Judaism.

So take a look around. Take a look at the person sitting next to you, at the team in the conference room, at the supplier visiting a contact, at your best customer. Are they ready to make this leap? Are you? What skills do you bring to the table? Do you care enough to make a difference? How do you join the revolution? Is there still time?

Here's some good news. There are specific practices that you can adopt to join in. In the next part of this book, I'll show you exactly how to become a revolutionary for good. You'll develop a solid foundation that will lead to breakthrough ideas. You'll benefit from the trial and error of the pioneers. You'll learn everything you need to know to be revolution-ready.

So join up and become a contributor to the balance sheet, the brand, and the future of your company. Most important, you will have the opportunity to save the world at work.

PART II

The Saver Soldier

8

The Six Laws of the Saver Soldier

In December 2006, footwear maker Timberland held its wholesale account reps sales rally in New Orleans, fifteen months after the city had been ravaged by Hurricane Katrina.

Timberland's event planners always inject a local community service component into the agenda, so on the conference's first evening, local leaders were asked to talk to the group about the battle to rebuild the city. On the second day, two hundred sales reps were taken by bus to New Orleans' historic Central City district to work on a neighborhood restoration program.

The specific project they were assigned to was renowned chef Dooky Chase's restaurant, a Central City neighborhood anchor, whose reopening meant a great deal to the area. So Timberlanders performed demolition, planted trees, hauled trash, and cleaned up a nearby playground, all working side by side with local volunteers.

In just a few hours, the Timberlanders made a difference in the restaurant and Central City's restoration. But feeling the reps needed to understand more about New Orleans' dismal situation, meeting planners decided to give them a tour of the Ninth Ward, one of the city's most devastated areas.

Jubilant while working so well at the Central City work site, the Timberlanders now became somber, realizing that even though one eatery had been spruced up, many parts of the city remained utterly uninhabitable.

At the end of the tour, the buses parked to allow the reps to get out and walk around the neighborhood. As they did, one rep noticed a makeshift community gathering spot constructed of tarps and rotted wood where a middle-aged man in a baseball cap was taking notes on a clipboard. The sales rep started a conversation with the man and soon discovered that he was a volunteer community organizer who had lived in the Ninth Ward pre-Katrina.

Moved by the moment, the rep asked the volunteer what the community center most needed.

"Shoes," the volunteer replied, pointing to a chalkboard that listed shoes at the top of the Please Drop Off list. "Used ones, new ones—we need shoes." He then explained that many of the community service volunteers were working in flip-flops and soleless shoes in an area littered with rusty nails and splintered boards.

The Timberland employee immediately bent down, unlaced his boots, and handed them to the volunteer. He then walked barefoot back to the buses, where employees were loading up for the ride back to the hotel.

A coworker, who noticed the sales rep wasn't wearing his boots, asked why. "That man there told me that they needed shoes," the sales rep replied, pointing to the community center. "I gave him mine."

The coworker stood up, left the bus, and gave the volunteer his shoes, too. The others watched, and acted: In the next ten minutes, the buses emptied out as all two hundred sales reps walked to the community center and donated their shoes or boots to the Ninth Ward, even though, for many of them, these Timberland boots were prized possessions.

The volunteer, overwhelmed, scrambled to keep pairs matched

together, tucking laces into boots and organizing them by size. All he could muster was a repetitive "Thank you, thank you" to every Timberlander.

The trip back to the hotel was silent, as employees reflected on what they'd seen that day. A senior meeting planner later recalled, "It was the quietest twenty-minute bus ride I've ever been on."

When the buses arrived at the hotel, the shoeless Timberlanders were stunned to find that, as they walked into the lobby, staff, guests, caterers, and cooks had gathered to give them a tearful reception, with hugs and handshakes. (One of the meeting planners had taken a picture of the donated shoes at the community center and sent it via cell phone to a coworker at the hotel.)

Over the next months, other Timberland employees became involved in the struggle to rebuild New Orleans. Furthermore, staff at the hotel and guests caught up in the moment were also inspired to do more to help out—in the Timberland culture, this is called a ripple: a single act that creates a chain reaction for good.

There are no names in this story: Timberland has a no-hero culture. The meeting planner who gave me the details of the story requested that she, along with the sales rep who first handed over his boots, remain anonymous.

"It doesn't matter who did it," the sales rep had said to her. "It just matters that it was done."

The people at Timberland are what I call *saver soldiers*. Joyce LaValle of Interface is also a saver soldier.

A saver soldier is a highly motivated individual who leverages work as a platform to help save the world. Some, like LaValle, want to help save the planet for humanity. Others want to free employees from unsafe working conditions, or rescue a local community from unacceptable levels of poverty, or protect endangered species, or save precious resources.

What all savers have in common is their belief that a business can do well by doing good. And they are driving that belief throughout their company.

Saver soldiers are the most important element inside a company helping to connect with the Responsibility Revolution. They consider their responsibility to encompass not just their cubicle and their office, but the world.

Saver CEOs such as Patagonia's Yvon Chouinard, Aveda's Horst Rechelbacher, and GE's Jeffrey Immelt have stated that they don't expect to achieve their vision single-handedly; they need foot soldiers to scout, innovate, and execute new ideas. Sometimes, as in the case of Interface, they don't even realize their company is on a crash course with the future—until someone like Joyce LaValle stands up and tells them so.

These saver soldiers are the drivers of many of the best ideas described throughout this book. Behind almost every landmark corporate social innovation you'll find a saver soldier who came up with a solution to a problem, then furiously sold it up to management for adoption.

While writing this book, I've talked to many dozens of saver soldiers and dissected their perspectives and day-to-day practices. From these insights, I've been able to harness easy-to-understand and easy-to-live-by strategies. I've isolated the successful approaches to distill a coherent curriculum. And I've tested strategies for both social value and long-term business acumen.

The following laws and advice points will help you achieve your dream of being an effective, change-the-world saver soldier.

Early savers, such as LaValle, acted intuitively—her success relied on a little luck and a great deal of effort. Many other potential savers want to make a difference but don't know how to effect real change. They don't understand the right way to approach the social problems they observe at work.

These points will help you avoid being stuck in that place. Instead, you will gain a solid sense of direction. Moreover, you'll discover how to effect changes in your company's strategy, regardless of your title and rank. You'll learn enough to be effective and to help teach these lessons to the future generations of socially minded professionals who cross your path.

The Six Laws of the Saver Soldier

Your personal transformation from businessperson to saver soldier begins with your perspective.

Your basic perception of the world, and which laws of biz-nature you choose to accept, will dictate many of your actions and reactions. An unenlightened outlook can impede your ability to make the right decisions, while an enlightened one will impart wisdom in situations where the average person wouldn't know what to do. Alan Kay, father of the personal computer, summed up the importance of outlook when he said, "Perspective is worth fifty IQ points."

Much like a computer, each of us has a basic operating system in our brain, our default setting, the one that guides us in our decision-making process, even when we're not aware we're making decisions.

This personal operating system, or OS, is shaped in large part by the beliefs that drive our actions. For example, if you believe "Buyers are liars," it will affect your outlook on prospective customers and influence how you behave toward them. If your OS says, "Knowledge is power," you may be programming yourself to withhold strategic information from other groups inside your company to bolster your own group's status.

One default outlook that many people hold is "Cover your ass (CYA)." This belief dictates how you respond to change. When an announcement appears regarding a new acquisition, product, or reorganization, a typical CYA response is "What does this mean to me?"

This is seldom a constructive reaction. For example, your boss tells you about a new company compensation plan designed to save money during tough times. If your knee-jerk response is to wonder, "How will this affect my paycheck?" you won't be seen as a team player.

Our personal OS is our choice. We aren't assigned an OS at birth, nor is there a rule that says we can't alter it. Although we may not be able to change our personality on a dime, we can take inventory of the business laws by which we live and chuck the ones that aren't beneficial.

I never thought about my beliefs in the first decade of my career. I just acted on them without thinking. Eventually, I learned that I couldn't be successful with the OS I had installed, which was based on the belief that this was a dog-eat-dog world and I won only when someone else lost.

As I learned more, however, I began to adopt a relationship-based perspective. In other words, I made a conscious decision to create a new belief system to guide my reaction to life's day-to-day challenges. It's something each of us can do.

1. The Law of the Ledger

Your company's financial success is always paramount—excellent fiscal acumen is fundamental to good business.

I first learned the Law of the Ledger in conversations with the late Stanley Marcus Jr. of Neiman Marcus. During the course of several lunches, we exchanged ideas; I talked about the digital economy, and he gave me advice about how to run a long-lasting business.

Marcus's department stores have long been recognized for promoting executives from within. Many employees have started as salespeople, become store managers within a few years, and eventually been promoted to corporate executive.

"How do you pick a good leader?" I once asked Marcus.

"I don't pick leaders," he replied. "I look for employees who are thoughtful of the ledger and mindful of the baby." His word for the company was always "baby."

Any employee who fully understands his or her contribution to the ledger, Marcus explained, is part of the solution and should be elevated to greater responsibilities.

In the store's early days, Mr. Marcus carried his business ledger everywhere he went, and he shared it with employees so they could see where they plugged into the puzzle. He showed them expenses, income, and assets. He looked for associates who understood this ledger and thoughtfully became a part of it. He taught them that no matter how big or mature Neiman Marcus became, it was still helpless to look after itself and depended on the stewardship of the ledger to survive and grow.

Finally, he explained that every business should require every employee to carry a "bag," a quantifiable contribution to the bottom line in either earnings, savings, or synergy. The ledger, the baby, the bag: These elements are the essence of business acumen.

Marcus taught me to think of your company as a baby who can't take care of itself. You are the baby's steward; you are accountable for your contributions and deductions from the ledger. If the ledger is in good shape, the baby is fed and prepared for a healthy future.

When you are hired, you accept an unspoken contract to contribute to the company's financial success. This contract must be met to make sure the bills are paid. Yes, good responsible business ensures customers tomorrow, but business acumen keeps the lights on today. If you ignore these business requirements, you are failing to keep your primary promise to the company.

Saver soldiers understand a company's short-, mid-, and long-term requirements for survival. They balance a sense of community with the realities of the day-to-day business world. This perspective allows saver soldiers to serve the company at the same time they serve the world.

Former Canon Corporation CEO Ryuzaburo Kaku, for example, believes that a strong business is the foundation of a good business. While at Canon, the large electronics maker, Kaku created a program of cooperation and social responsibility called *Kyosei*, which he describes as "a spirit of cooperation in which individuals and organizations live and work together for the common good."

Kyosei committed Canon to engage in effective and ethical business practices, while leveraging the company's resources to help tackle world problems from poverty to blindness. In his *Harvard Business Review* essay "The Path to *Kyosei*," Kaku reminded readers, "To support this ideal, a corporation must naturally create wealth and fulfill its financial production role [what Stanley Marcus would call the credit side of the balance sheet]. The *Kyosei* journey begins by laying a sound business foundation, securing predictable streams of profits."

The Law of the Ledger aligns those who want to help their companies do good in the world with the existing management team, and maintains your credibility as a responsible employee as you look for ways to save the world at work. In fact, displaying business acumen will make you more influential as you align yourself with senior executives.

Those who lack business acumen cannot be true saver soldiers.

Companies in economic crisis can't worry about the environment, the future, or their employees. Bad numbers create bad business. If your company isn't making money, it can't be expected to help anyone.

2. The Law of Interdependence

This law states that, for the most part, the strength of a business depends on the strength of the greater community.

Interdependence, a term gleaned from science, describes the relationships among all living organisms. We live in an ecosystem composed of four interrelated systems: biophysical, economic, social, and political. Each system's success or failure is tied to the fate of the other three—that is, a breakdown in the biophysical environment will create significant hardships in economic, political, and social systems, and so on.

Interdependence in a business context implies that a company is part of a greater ecosystem—comprising myriad stakeholders, other companies, communities, governments, and the natural environment. In such a system, a small ripple can create dramatic waves. (A stakeholder is any person, group, or entity that contributes to and can be affected by a company's actions or outcomes.)

Today, when the Euronext Index burps, the Pacific Stock Exchange hiccups. When the Chinese stock market takes a dive, your mutual fund shrinks accordingly. A child-labor crackdown in Brazil leads to a disruption in the supply chain of PVC joints to manufacturers in Ireland, which in turn leads to a price hike on plumbing supplies throughout the southern United States. That is interdependence in action.

Interdependence can be observed on a local level as well. In 1996, UPS realized that it was running out of qualified job candidates in one of its major hub cities, Louisville, Kentucky. Although unemployment was at an all-time high, graduation rates had dipped dramatically over a twenty-year period and few graduates had the means to pursue higher education. The available job pool didn't have the level of education that UPS needed.

UPS then invested in School-to-Work, a program offered to high school seniors that provided work experience, as well as college credits, through corporate-funded courses. The program steered graduates to Metropolitan College, where their education was paid for as long as they continued to work at UPS.

As a result, UPS has gained thousands of strong, committed employees with college degrees and practical skills ranging from accounting to public speaking. As Mike Eskew, former CEO of UPS, says: "If they do well, we do well."

The reverse is also true: Your town depends on your company's success, down to the last citizen. In the early 2000s, when Houston-based energy company Enron failed, its employees lost their livelihood. The pain didn't stop there. From coffee-shop owners to shoe shiners, thousands of locals who didn't work for Enron lost their jobs too, not to mention the pain felt by innumerable retirees across the country whose mutual funds were invested in Enron stock.

In today's global economy, no company is independent of the outside world. Interface's Saver CEO Anderson says: "A company is a wholly owned subsidiary of the planet." A crash in the ecosystem will decimate your company's business prospects. The planet provides essential services every business needs: breathable oxygen, potable water, energy for heat and power, natural resources, habitable living conditions. If any of these vanish, as happened in post-Katrina New Orleans, businesses feel the pain.

Your company has an interdependent relationship with its employees and the host communities where it does business as well. If the people who work for and with you fell ill and called in sick, who would run the business? If your community collapsed under the weight of a failing infrastructure, poor schools, or the devastation of poverty, where would your company get the services it needs? These are some of the questions companies must ask when faced with business decisions that potentially harm people, the surrounding community, or the planet.

Businesses must look at the effect of their decisions on all their stakeholders, not just investors or owners. Employees, partners, suppliers, customers, communities, and the ecosystem all depend on management's thoughtfulness.

The ThemGeners have learned that no decision exists in a vacuum. As consumers, they will punish companies that behave contrary to their beliefs. By realigning on the right side of the responsibility revolution, companies can create a style of business that resonates with the times.

3. The Law of Abundance

The Law of Abundance essentially states that there is always enough to go around. There are enough customers, enough talented people, enough recognition, enough of whatever is needed. Based on his research into personal effectiveness, bestselling author Dr. Stephen Covey suggests that we would all be more effective if we developed the abundance mentality: "It opens possibilities, alternatives, and creativity."

People who possess an abundance mentality can find contentment where others find envy. Let's say you work at a company where another business unit has received a large research-and-development budget. Rather than feeling envious or rejected, those who see life from the vantage point of abundance choose to be happy, because the money is beneficial to the entire company and all will ultimately profit.

Suppose your biggest competitor figures out a way to produce its product in a much greener way, reducing its environmental impact without increasing price or lowering quality. The media respond by showering the company with accolades. For those who believe in abundance, this is a win/win for everyone. Those driven by the scarcity mind-set, however, will focus on why the idea will not work for you, or worse, denigrate it as greenwash propaganda.

People with a scarcity mind-set resent others' successes, even those of their own teammates. For them, life is a zero-sum game: If one person wins, another loses.

In the business world, the Law of Abundance suggests that companies and individuals can find ways to solve pressing social needs, whether the problem requires money, resources, or time. Why? Because such companies and individuals believe that this way of thinking will ultimately lead to more money (fresh customers), more knowledge (valuable feedback and information from grateful clients and customers), and more time (as recipients of your generosity reciprocate the favor and offer their resources in the future).

I see abundance thinkers as Big Pie People. They know the pie of life is big enough for everyone to get a slice. They're the ones who discuss possibilities instead of limitations. They approach every shortage as a creative challenge. They never think, to quote poet Robert Lowell, that "the light at the end of the tunnel is just the light of an oncoming train."

We should all be Big Pie People. We can all create a bigger pie rather than fight over who gets which piece. The basic unit of business value creation is no longer limited by raw materials such as steel, land, or fuel. Today, the basic building blocks of business growth are bits, not bricks; it is based on intellectual capital, not just capital.

Futurist Alvin Toffler calls today's era "the Third Wave," the wave of information. "For the Third Wave civilization," Toffler writes, "the most basic raw material of all, and one that can never be exhausted, is information, including imagination. Through imagination and information, substitutes will be found for many of today's exhaustible resources."

The information superhighway offers a solution to the dependence on scarce resources, especially when it comes to business needs. Banks such as ING Direct or E-Trade Inc., which would have previously required brick-and-mortar locations, exist almost entirely online and are growing faster than their land-based rivals. Factory managers employ waste-reduction programs to stretch their energy supplies to more than meet their needs. Retail stores expand their shelf space to infinity with Web-based locations. Hospitals tap into an endless stream of global experts and specialists via high-speed Internet video connections. A material shortfall is just an issue that needs to be addressed with information and imagination. With ideas, anything is possible.

The abundance mentality works on a personal and professional level, too. A great idea remains worthless as long as you hold on to it. But if you share it with your colleagues, your idea grows more valuable over time. You gain valuable feedback, which more often than not improves the idea.

The Law of Abundance allows you to become a problem solver instead of a corporate Chicken Little. You see possibilities rather than deficiencies. You look for synergy instead of division in your business dealings. You give instead of take, because when you feel like you have plenty, something inside you says to give something back. Over time, you'll find your attitude rubbing off on your colleagues, employees, and teammates, creating a feeling that together anything can be solved.

While working for CEO Mark Cuban at Broadcast.com in 1999, I witnessed the power of choosing to think in terms of abundance rather than scarcity—especially in times of great change.

When broadcast.com was sold to Yahoo!, two tribes formed inside the company: the "We gained something" group and the "We lost something" group. The latter group responded to the acquisition with fear and regret, afraid that their titles would be downgraded and that they'd lose their autonomy. The more this group talked amongst themselves, the more upset they became. The Yahoos found them very off-putting and few survived at the company for more than a year.

Meanwhile, the "We gained something" group chose to see the acquisition through the lens of abundance creation. Before, we had 1 million monthly visitors, but now we had 100 million. And when it came to resources, we had four hundred more engineers available to help us solve problems and serve customers. Moreover, we believed Yahoo!'s brand would bring us more authority in the market and, over time, more expansive budgets. Many who fell into this group, including myself, were transferred to California and given bigger responsibilities.

The choice to view life through the lens of abundance will give you confidence to be generous and cooperative during good times and bad. Think about when you are charitable on a personal level, donating money to worthy causes or giving time to help out your community. You do it because you believe that there's enough to go around. We all need to take this belief to work.

4. The Law of Reciprocity
The Law of Reciprocity states that people will give back when they've been given to.

For the most part, every time you do the right thing for your customers, employees, partners, and/or greater community, these people will find a way to repay you, through loyalty, by giving thoughtful feedback to improve your business, by telling their friends to buy from you or to work at your company.

As Adam Smith, the grandfather of Western economic philosophy, wrote in *The Theory of Moral Sentiments*: "No benevolent man ever lost altogether the fruits of his benevolence. If he doesn't always gather them from the persons from whom he ought to have gathered them, he seldom fails to gather them from other people, and with a tenfold increase. Kindness is the parent of kindness."

Since Smith, thousands of equally intelligent people have made similar claims. Yet we often find the Law of Reciprocity difficult to believe. This doubt is due in part to the fact that we grossly exaggerate the number of times people don't repay our thoughtfulness. We hate to be wrong about making bets on people, so when it happens, we remember those incidents much more vividly than those in which people pay our kindness back with kindness.

But adherence to this law actually expands our ability to trust people and make investments in them. We develop informed faith and a purposeful sense of trust in people's nature; we make a leap and put our money on people doing the right thing in the long run; we believe goodwill eventually produces profits and revenue.

Several years ago Jim Goodnight, CEO of SAS Institute, asked me to speak at a leadership event for his company in Las Vegas. One night Jim took my wife, Jacqueline, and me to a casino, and although Goodnight is a billionaire, he searched high and low for a five-dollar blackjack table. When he found one, he gambled one chip at a time, despite the fact that he had developed a winning mathematical formula.

Given his wealth, I asked Jim why he bet so conservatively. "I make all my big bets on my people," he replied.

Make an informed bet on a person at work and note his or her inclination to give back. If you're a manager, make a bet on one of your direct reports. If you're a clerk, take a gamble on a coworker. If you're a purchasing agent, make an investment in a supplier. I believe you will find, more often than not, that the other person will recognize and appreciate your investment and make an attempt to reciprocate.

You may even find that they outgive you. For example, when you invest time in mentoring an employee, you may well discover that he or she gives back multiples of your investment in time, effort, and effectiveness.

5. The Law of the Long View

The Law of the Long View states that while making any decision, you must consider its long-term implications.

Long-view thinking considers various consequences in response to an act over time.

There are several ways to implement long-view thinking; one is to look into the future and consider chain reactions to business activity. Interface's Ray Anderson always asks the question "And then what happens?" when conducting a review of any products or practices his staff is pitching.

Long viewers gaze beyond the quarter and into the future where, for example, pollution or carbon emissions may show up as collateral damage from past actions. They are likely to believe in community development, because over time it will produce expanded markets and vendor options. They are likely to favor training and development for their employees, because they understand the long-term benefits that stem from on-the-job education.

Another way to incorporate the long view into your thinking is to engage in scenario planning. Scenario planning is an exercise that requires participants to imagine a different world based on five- to ten-year projections: What might the world look like, what kind of rules might the world live by, and what values might the future world hold?

This practice emerged as a business exercise run by Pierre Wack, who oversaw Royal Dutch/Shell's strategic planning team in the 1970s. Wack required that his managers create at least two different worlds that could exist in five years, and then project how current plans would play out in those worlds. As Peter Schwartz said in his book *The Art of the Long View,* "Wack was not interested in predicting the future. His goal was the liberation of people's insights."

Such liberation is critical in helping us break free from the shackles of short-term thinking. Many of us may have been taught to think of only today's world when making business decisions. Yet a change in context can create new and often unforeseen possibilities. By focusing on potential tomorrows, we think like social innovators.

This is why Toyota made its bold move into hybrid-car technology. Back in the mid-1990s, company planners and executives dreamed up a world in which consumers became environmentally aware and viewed reducing their carbon footprint as a matter of pride. The planners also imagined a world of increased demand for oil, driving the price of gas beyond three dollars a gallon.

Based on this view, Toyota launched the Prius. They took a short-term hit on earnings and industry pundits laughed. Today, they are an industry leader in the fast-growing area of hybrid-engine technology. Ford now licenses technology from Toyota while short-term thinkers from GM to BMW scramble to play catch-up.

It can feel problematic to take a longer view at work. Our operating systems are programmed to focus on the quarterly report or the average manager's annual view. Scenarios that will unfold over a decade are seldom encouraged in the rush-rush world of modern business.

We live in a cell phone—BlackBerry—e-mail—instant gratification culture in which everybody wants an answer a minute ago. Living in this right-now world erodes our ability to look ahead, so instead of creating future scenarios, we're putting out fires and moving on to the next thing on our to-do list. This practice rarely builds great businesses. Taking the long view is a courageous choice, one that will expand your value to your business as well as to society. Once you put on long-view glasses, you can see all the ramifications of a business decision over time. Such vision can enable you to protect your company's reputation, avoiding future harm to people, communities, and the planet, making it critical to a company's survival in the Responsibility Revolution.

As Peter Schwartz writes, "Companies that take the short view are quite frequently disrupted by changes in the context of business that they never dreamed of."

The long view can also protect you from coming up with a social innovation that turns out to be damaging—after all, sometimes ideas created with the best intentions don't work over the long haul.

For example, Paul Margolis, one of the founders of Atlantis Solutions, a West Coast computer services company, had a noble idea: Give away one-third of company profits to local charities. The company had high profit margins and wanted to make a contribution at a local level. Community leaders applauded the move and encouraged business owners to go out of their way to support them.

However, increased competition slowly shrunk Atlantis's margins, and the company had very little cash on hand to respond to much larger competitors that had entered their market with lower-priced services and massive marketing programs. The company was forced to cancel its philanthropic plan, enraging local officials.

Atlantis then laid off more than a hundred employees in a belt-tightening move. With little cash on hand and a reputation for being disloyal, the company went into a tailspin and had to shut down operations. Hundreds of employees lost their jobs. In the long run, the company's noble idea failed to account for a world with more competition and lower profit margins.

The same circumstances can develop around the best-intentioned environmental ambitions. For example, campaigns that focus solely on recycling paper often fail to take into account how workers might respond to such an initiative. Recycling is generally thought of as a panacea—workers believe that it is fine to print out as many copies of documents as they want, as long as the company recycles. Over the long run, though, recycling consumes petroleum and electricity, and rescues only a small percentage of paper for future use.

The long view gives Responsibility Revolutionaries a necessary ingredient for success—vision. Many bad ideas are good ideas that fail to look past the present balance sheet or press release. The long view can help separate intentions from reality. You don't want to be just well-intentioned. You want to make a difference. Only time can reveal the difference between the two.

6. The Law of the Last Mile

The Law of the Last Mile states that if you don't finish what you start, you might as well not start at all. The only way to add true social value is to finish the difficult last mile.

In business, the term "last mile" describes the final few action items required to convert an idea into a reality. When launching a new product, for example, the last mile is getting it into the hands of the customer.

The term originated in the telecom business to describe the last leg of connectivity between a company's network and its customers. Due to the complexity of fanning out wires to homes, this leg was frequently the bottleneck. The old saying went, "If your customers don't hear a dial tone, you aren't in business as far as they're concerned."

Likewise, if your company launches a program to distribute food to the homeless in your community, the last mile is getting the food to the hungry. No matter how many people are involved, no matter how many cans of corn you collect, if you don't ensure that the corn makes it into someone's hands, no one cares, and no one eats.

Social-responsibility initiatives are often complicated and involve many steps between creation and completion. Few produce any value if they are not 100 percent implemented. Projects based on objectives require, above all else, execution.

Many times we are deluded into believing that true innovation is simply a matter of spotting a problem and coming up with a creative solution to it. But thinking up a solution isn't enough. Remember professor Henry Chesbrough's definition of innovation: an idea successfully brought to market.

Most projects fail because they get bogged down in that last mile. Unlike the first few miles, in which the team is inspired and has yet to encounter obstacles, the last mile is fraught with difficult details. People run out of gas, they lose sight of their objective, they find that the last mile resembles Zeno's paradox—you keep getting closer and closer to the finish line, but you never quite seem to make it.

Saver soldiers who start but don't finish often do more harm than good. Intending to make a difference, they create problems for future saver soldiers. The failure to finish generates cynicism. This is especially true when it comes to socially responsible programs.

Say a company announces that it will practice fair trade, using only products from producers who pay a living wage and have humane working conditions. Its last mile might be a program to verify supplier compliance. If this doesn't happen, and word gets out that the company isn't 100 percent behind its promise, a backlash ensues. When another company makes the same announcement a few years later, people bring doubts to the table and the new initiative fails to enhance the company's reputation.

This process applies at an individual level as well. Let's say a human resources staffer creates a cultural health initiative, a data-driven program designed to ensure employee satisfaction with the work environment. Making the announcement is fun. Building the survey to measure satisfaction is exciting. Rolling out the survey to the employee base generates a rewarding buzz.

The last mile is to implement policy changes in response to the data gathered. Now the rubber hits the road. Say it's hard to schedule meetings with executives, managers are resistant to change, the HR team becomes discouraged, and no policy changes occur. Then, a few years later, a new HR staffer announces a similar initiative.

Everyone in the company rolls their eyes: "Here we go again." The program doesn't stand a chance. By failing to finish, the former staffer has sealed the fate of other initiatives as well for a long time to come.

To be an effective saver soldier, you must take responsibility for the last mile. In his book *The Project 50*, author Tom Peters suggests that every project team elect a Mr./Ms. Last-Two-Percent to ensure completion. This person's finishing fanaticism can mean the difference between success and failure.

By focusing on the last mile, you will dramatically increase your chances of making a difference, now and into the future. The last mile may not be easy to finish, but it is the one that counts most.

PART III

The Practice of
Being Good

9

Assess

It's time to move from thinking to doing. Saver soldiers are people of action. When presented opportunities to add social value, savers seize them.

Back in 2000, I worked with Tim Koogle, former CEO of Yahoo! and, before that, an executive at Motorola during the Quality Revolution. Koogle taught me many significant lessons, including the value of being a person of action. He used to say that we should be wary of people who live in the "ing state," people who are always study*ing*, think*ing*, meet*ing*, or talk*ing*. In his view, such people were a waste of time and energy.

Instead, he encouraged us to seek out partners who lived in the "ed state": people who have execut*ed*, complet*ed*, and act*ed*. The most effective business partners do their best to fulfill their intentions.

In this section, you will discover dozens of ways you can act to help your company do well by doing good, leveraging work as a platform to make a difference. Along the way, you'll also learn how to help position your company for success during the Responsibility Revolution.

I believe the result will be success for you and your company as you help to add social value for key stakeholders: employees, suppliers, customers, investors, communities, and the environment.

According to a multiyear study released in 2006 by market research company Golin-Harris, the public measures a company's social responsibility by the quality of its relationships with each of its stakeholders. If a company undervalues or harms any one of them, it isn't acting responsibly.

This view is based on a sense of fairness and ethics—the belief that these stakeholders provide a company with the resources necessary to operate and thrive. Employees offer the skills and effort required to execute a company's business plan. Suppliers contribute vital business resources to deliver value to customers. Customers provide cash flow, feedback, and word-of-mouth marketing. Investors give the company its operating capital. Communities host companies, providing services, customers, and employees. The environment provides resources, including air, water, light, stable weather, and raw materials.

(Ecological economist Robert Costanza has estimated the economic contribution of nature's services to be more than $33 trillion, a sum greater than the economic value of human services.)

You now have a blueprint for success as a saver: Serve stakeholders in your daily business life. From this point forward, your job will be to reduce the harm and maximize the social value your company delivers to each stakeholder, all of whom should be in better condition because of the existence of your company—and you.

Assess Your Company

First things first. To start on the journey of becoming an effective saver, first assess your company's current place on the responsibility continuum and place it within the context of the Responsibility Revolution.

Go online. Google your company. Don't just search for the company name—add a series of keywords and phrases, such as *lawsuit, social responsibility, safety, fair trade, awards, protest, injustice, sustainability*, and *liability*.

Next, go to Hoovers.com, a popular business research Web site that provides analysis for investors, and search for reports on your company. If your company is public, you can also try Yahoo! Finance, TheStreet.com, or MSN Money, where you will find news items and SEC filings, as well as a bulletin board. Many of the board comments won't be accurate, but if you notice consistent patterns of complaints, from mistreating workers to polluting a water system, take note and do more research.

See if any blogs talk about your company's social performance—Google and Yahoo! both offer blog search features, or try blogsearch.com. Look through the newspaper in the town where the company is headquartered. Local papers have a keen interest in companies in their market, often leading the charge in both positive and negative coverage. Search out the bad news as well as the good—the negative news can help you calculate the social costs your company creates as well as its reputation as a corporate citizen.

Another indicator of a company's reputation is the presence of large, well-organized groups critical of your company such as www.untied.com, which protests poor treatment of fliers by United Airlines, or watchdog groups such as www.walmartwatch.com, which reports on the huge retailer.

Read what such detractors say with an open mind. Some of these groups' claims may be baseless; what you are looking for are widely held beliefs about your company that signal a problem worthy of further consideration.

Now it's time to look at some of the good news about your com-

pany: its accomplishments, awards, philanthropy, outreach programs, or other signs of a positive reputation, such as being ranked
by *Business Ethics* or *CRO* magazine as a top corporate citizen.

Start at your company's Web site; examine its corporate social-
responsibility section. Almost all Fortune 1000 companies aggregate
the company's positive contributions here. Thousands of companies
also produce annual sustainability reports covering these accomplishments, usually offered online along with the annual financial
report.

Investigate further. Is your company a "make-waste organization," as Interface's Ray Anderson puts it? Do you see wasteful behavior? Are your company's policies sensible?

Does your company have a culture of compassion, or one of mere
efficiency? Observe the interactions between management and employees, and between individual supervisors and their direct reports.

Does your company pay its employees a living wage? Do employees have health care coverage—or are they spending entire
weekends at the free clinic because that's all they can afford? Try to
get a sense of how competitive your company is in terms of wages
and benefits.

Penn State University hosts a free living-wage Web calculator at
www.livingwage.geog.psu.edu. It shows how much employees need
to make to survive, based on where they live and the size of their
families. How do you think your company fares against its competitors in the area?

Is much of your company's staff part-time? This strategy can be
effective in cutting costs, but does so by excluding employees from
health coverage and other benefits. Most companies, especially those
in the retail and food-service businesses, offer benefits only to full-
time employees; part-timers seldom receive sick or vacation days,
personal-development training, or a host of other benefits full-

timers enjoy. Many retailers also rely on flexible schedules to manage their workforce around times when retail traffic is heaviest. But they do so with complete disregard to the impact on their employees.

Does your company have don't-ask-don't-tell concerns, such as harassment of those who look or act different? Is your company inclusive of all orientations, cultures, and beliefs, and is respect for this diversity universal? Find out if your company offers same-sex domestic-partner benefits, an acid test of responsibility for Them-Geners.

Next, do you know how your company acquires the supplies that make its business run? Do the buyers ask questions beyond price or quality? Is there a mission-aligned review of new products? What is the nature of the company's vendor relations? Some overly efficient companies can be brutal to their vendors, forcing them to cut corners to reduce the cost of their materials, squeezing profits and wages for those farther down the line.

Now evaluate the relationship between your company and your local community. Is your company a partner or a parasite? Does it rely on the community for resources—health care, infrastructure—yet ignore its problems?

The last piece of your assessment involves your competitors: What are they doing in the social arena? Google them and read up on their social responsibility accomplishments. Visit their Web sites. Like your company, your competitors may devote sections of their sites to community outreach, diversity, the environment, and so on. How would you sum up their social reputation? Are they considered innovators or laggards? Compare their efforts to your own company's efforts. Is your company ahead of or behind the competition in the Responsibility Revolution?

With your research in hand, it's time to create a total social assessment of your company. When it comes to your company's interaction with employees, community, and the environment, what should it stop doing? What should it start doing? Which of its positive actions should be continued, improved, or amplified? Make a list; it will prove handy later as you dive into the specific practices you may want to address.

Your assessment will also help you better understand what you can do as a saver. For example, if your assessment suggests your company is creating long-term environmental damage, as Joyce La-Valle realized Interface was doing, you will want to be a change agent to help green up operations.

Similarly, if you realize that your company skimps on health benefits or mistreats its employees, you may want to focus your efforts on changing your company's corporate policies.

Don't limit your thinking to areas of the company where you feel you have some control; that is, never write off an area for change because of your lack of a title or rank. I'll show you later that we all have the power to change anything we choose at our companies.

On the other hand, if your assessment shows that you're working at a company that is a pioneer or innovator, perhaps your role should be that of a booster, supporting existing efforts and initiatives.

However, remember that even the best-run and best-intentioned companies can lose their way as a result of changes in ownership or leadership, market conditions, and/or employee participation. I believe the general public will be unforgiving to companies that go back on their word as good corporate citizens.

To ensure that your company stays on track, participate in corporate programs aimed at developing people, community, and the planet.

10

Act: Save Your People

Every one of us can jump into the revolution right now by bettering our company's social performance. You can improve the quality of life for your company's people. You can add value to the communities in which you do business. You can help protect the environment for future generations. It's just a question of identifying an opportunity and then acting.

There are dozens of opportunities to help save the world at work. Please don't think you have to do everything on the list, however—this is only a starting point for social innovation.

Many of the tips I'm suggesting are within your reach in your current role at work, whatever it is. Chances are you manage others, even if just a few. And if you don't have people reporting to you yet, you likely will in the next few years. Researchers at Gallup estimate that seven out of ten professionals will manage others at some point in their career.

Think about the ideas on the list that follows that make the most sense for you, and only you. Some of these suggestions may even spur you to invent other opportunities. Helping to reduce paper consumption, for example, may not fit your industry, but it may trigger ideas about an associated issue. When you can make that type of connection, you're thinking like an innovator.

You may look through the list of recommendations and decide to take on a single area of innovation. Many savers choose to innovate in one area and execute it very well.

Pick your battles carefully. Calculate how much time you'll need for an action item and make enough room for it in your schedule. Be willing to commit personal time, if necessary, to the task. If you see an opportunity to make a difference, do it right away.

When you spot a suggestion that appeals to you but isn't within your purview, put it on your wish list of revolutionary changes you'd like to see at your company. These may be something you can do down the road.

People

The first place the public looks to determine whether a company is socially responsible is its treatment of its people. (When I say a company's "people," I include its employees, contract workers, partners, customers, and shareholders.) Regardless of how many people with whom you come in contact, every one of them should be better off for having known you and your company.

According to the Golin-Harris study, valuing and treating employees "well and fairly" is the top driver of a company's social reputation; a 2006 survey conducted by Fleishman-Hillard for the National Consumers League found that nearly half of Americans say that "treating and paying employees well is the most important proof of good corporate social responsibility, more so than environmental stewardship and philanthropy."

Simply going green, or supporting charities, isn't enough. Your company will lag behind the innovators if it drops the ball on employee relations. "If companies want to maintain and strengthen their reputations," says Fleishman-Hillard CEO John Graham, "it will be essential for them to invest actively and visibly in their employees."

A good saver soldier begins the battle here, at the intersection of company and employee.

The first eight suggestions here apply to anyone, regardless of title or role; the last six apply specifically to managers and supervisors.

1. Join a Corporate Mentorship Program

Corporate mentorship programs help employees become more successful at the company and lay the foundation for flourishing careers. Most companies offer at least some form of it, usually within the human resources department.

Sun Microsystems' program, called Sun Engineering Enrichment Development, matches high-potential employees with senior engineers in a one-year arrangement in which both parties spend a few hours together weekly. According to Sun, program mentees earn four times more promotions than the average employee, and receive performance ratings twice as good.

General Mills' Corporate Diversity Mentoring program is designed to match new hires of color to senior-level employees; the program successfully promotes diversity by helping minority participants master the corporate culture. Professional services company Ernst & Young offers a Women's Access Program, where partners are matched with female managers to promote their careers.

One of the most socially innovative programs is Hallmark's Compassionate Connections, in which employees going through stressful life events are matched with other employees who've experienced similar situations.

The easiest way to find a mentorship opportunity is to log on to your corporate intranet and click on Human Resources. Most HR intranet sites have a category called Training and Development, where you'll find such mentorship programs. At companies such as Intel Corporation and DuPont, online tools effectively match mentors and mentees, based on qualifications versus needs. You can also use the intranet's search engine to look for terms such as "mentorship program" and "knowledge sharing" and "ambassador program."

2. Mentor a Coworker or Employee

If your company doesn't have a mentorship program, think about creating one yourself.

Is there someone with whom you work in close proximity to whom you can offer professional, technical, financial, leadership, or personal advice? You came up through the ranks; perhaps you can help others avoid pitfalls.

The key is to treat others with empathy and respect. Let potential mentees know you want to help them by sharing your knowledge and skills. Don't act as if you want to "fix" them or, worse, make it seem that they sorely need help. Project engagement, not intimidation.

Take your mentee under your wing for at least a few months. Measure his or her progress and take special note of advice that leads to action. If your mentee is making progress, renew your commitment. In my experience, it can take a year or more to fully share your advice and experience. Give yourself, and the person you are mentoring, plenty of time.

Finally, make it clear to your mentees that their only obligation is to pay the help forward to others rather than repay you. This process will help to grow a mentorship culture inside your company.

Mentorship can change people's lives. I learned this firsthand when I was mentored in the late 1990s while working at Broadcast.com.

Because the company was a start-up, mentorship was more of a management practice than a formal human resources program. Each manager was expected to mentor high-potential, but struggling, people.

In 1998, Rick Jackson, a former EDS sales director, was hired to run the business services group, where I'd been working as an account executive for six months. With only a handful of sales, I was in danger of losing my job.

Jackson singled me out for mentorship because he had faith that, with a little coaching and training, I could be one of his top sales reps. First, he taught me how to use ACT, a popular contacts and time-management software program. Previous to that, I'd used a paper-based Day-Timer. By adopting ACT, I doubled my productivity.

Next, he mentored me in presentation skills, showing me how to use PowerPoint. To track my sales progress, he taught me how to use Excel, Microsoft Office's spreadsheet.

Jackson also taught me how to sell business services to corporate buyers properly, by helping me to understand how to calculate how much money my prospects would save with our services. Until then, like most rookies in the business, I was selling the features (bells and whistles) of the service instead of the financial benefits that it had to offer.

Broadcast.com was in the business of webcasting live events, and the technology was far from perfect. The last area of mentorship Jackson covered was crisis management—how to manage client expectations and keep everyone's head cool when something went wrong with the webcast. By mastering these skills, I was promoted to director of business development and placed in charge of handling some of the biggest deals (and crises) at the company.

After Yahoo! bought Broadcast.com in 1998, Jackson arranged for me to give a presentation on the future of webcasting at a quarterly sales meeting for the company in Dallas, where several key

Yahoo! executives were in attendance. Because that presentation was successful, I was offered a promotion and transferred to corporate headquarters.

Even though he was no longer my boss, Jackson continued to advise me on the politics of moving up in the company. I owe much of my success at Yahoo! to his advice; without it, I wouldn't be writing this book.

3. Integrate a New Person into the Company

Don't let the newbies feel abandoned. The first day on the job can be frightening; even companies that spend a great deal of money to wine and dine a candidate before he or she takes the job can leave that person feeling helpless during the first week at the office.

Savers don't let this happen. They take matters into their own hands and help the newbies create necessary and valuable connections.

This is especially true during an acquisition. If someone works for a company that's been swallowed, he or she can feel lost within the new giant. The transition period offers a wonderful opportunity for you to make an immediate difference.

To help the newbies network, first find out what they are working on, as well as their business interests and passions. Organize an informal lunch or coffee break with a handful of coworkers who might be good contacts. If you don't have much time, introduce them via an e-mail, making it clear why you think everyone would benefit by meeting. Take advantage of how well you know the company. Don't hesitate to make cross-company introductions, jumping from one business unit to another, because these are usually the types of introductions newbies have trouble making on their own.

The more you help the newbies network, the more quickly they

will become engaged at work and integrated into the corporate culture. There are potential rewards for you as well—such as growing
your own network: Many of today's newbies are tomorrow's leaders.

4. Help Coworkers in Need

One of the best ways to connect your company to its people is to make
their problems your problems.

Sometimes people just need to be able to talk to someone else.
They may be feeling upset and stressed, unable to imagine that anyone else in the world could understand their pain. Simply by listening, you can ease that suffering. Now they know they're not alone.

Other people don't need an ear but a helping hand. Many companies overtax employees. If you have a little free time, jump in and
help. Your willingness to step forward can make all the difference.

Your generosity will reinforce the Law of Abundance as you realize that there's enough to go around. This is one of the great benefits
of being charitable: It proves that by giving, you'll gain. And you'll
have contributed to your company's results and culture by teaching
abundance to those around you.

When we accept others' problems as our own and become part of
the solution, we also reinforce the Law of Interdependence—the fact
that all our needs and hopes are intertwined.

5. Give Ample Recognition

Charles M. Schwab, the turn-of-the-century steel magnate, practiced recognition daily. When asked the secret of his success in
managing others, he replied, "I'm hearty with my approbation and
lavish with praise."

In an era and an industry where labor generally toiled in unsafe
and thankless conditions, Schwab offered an emotional oasis to

workers and managers, attracting top talent as a result. His recruitment and motivation skills eventually led him to the presidency of
Bethlehem Steel.

Part of Schwab's success derived from his ability to give people
what they wanted: recognition. That need is universal and timeless.
More than ever, people define themselves by their jobs and how well
they do them. When they don't receive acknowledgment for their efforts, their sense of self-worth is diminished.

Recognition can be professional and personal. Professional recognition acknowledges an employee's contribution to the company's
success, from hitting a sales target to going beyond the norm in
helping a client or customer to provide an innovative solution to a
problem.

Personal recognition rewards an employee's efforts and accomplishments outside of his or her job, such as completing a college
degree, winning a civic award, or performing an act of compassion
or heroism. Here, too, recognition at the office makes a difference,
no matter what other acknowledgment has been received.

One low-tech way to reward others uses a favorite corporate pas-
time: writing on whiteboards with dry erase markers. This is what
the IT group at the British Columbia Lottery System did after a manager put up a "Recognition Whiteboard" in the office commons.
Thereafter, anyone could scribble notes of recognition for other
team members. Introverted techies found the whiteboard a great
way to thank each other for contributions to a project's success.

Why not put one of these up at your office with a title such as
"Shout Outs," "Rock Stars on Campus," or, simply, "The Recognition Board." Get the party started by posting some thank-yous.

Some companies offer recognition opportunities on their corporate intranet. See if your company already has one. If so, contrib-

ute to the conversation next time. E-mail links to it to your project partners or teammates.

If you're a manager, be sure to lavish recognition, whenever deserved, on your reports. I call one approach the "quarterly one plus one": Every ninety days, strive to give one personal and one professional compliment to the people who work with and for you. Again, be specific and authentic.

Some managers recognize their employees' work anniversary. This is a person's business birthday—the moment he or she entered the company culture. This day possesses personal significance to many people, so it's a terrific opportunity to let them know the difference they've made to the company or to you.

Make sure you give recognition to everyone who deserves it, not just to people you like or notice. Some managers make a practice of asking, "Who else helped you accomplish this?" When they find out the others connected to the contribution, they extend recognition there, too.

Corporate events offer a great venue for recognizing an individual's accomplishments on a large scale. Here's an example: Marty Dillon, a tax professional at H&R Block, needed a kidney for his daughter, Alison. As time was running out, he posted a flyer at work hoping to find a volunteer.

Lisa Millard, a regional marketing director, saw the flyer and was intrigued. She had already signed up to be an organ donor after her death but hadn't realized it was possible to be a living donor.

Millard's dog, her companion for more than a decade, had just died, and she had no one else special in her life, nor did her family have any kidney problems that might require a gift. Finally, as it was fall and tax season didn't heat up again until the first of the year, she'd have time to recuperate.

Millard contacted Dillon and began the donation process at Westchester Medical Center in Valhalla, New York. The doctors and nurses there were startled that Millard would give her kidney to a coworker's daughter—until then, the hospital had never witnessed a non–family member organ donation. They were more amazed to discover that Millard didn't know the recipient; she intentionally avoided contact with Alison because she didn't want to discover anything that might dissuade her.

In September of 2007, Millard donated her kidney in a successful procedure.

Although she didn't talk about the incident, word spread and the story made its way back to H&R Block corporate headquarters.

A few months later, after speaking at the company's annual management conference, I watched Millard receive a service award in front of a thousand of her peers—most of whom were crying. Several of her close coworkers remarked that until that moment, they hadn't even heard about it.

Many studies have shown that when you witness, or hear about, an act of compassion, you're more likely to emulate it. Millard's story had that effect on the H&R Block audience. Dozens of H&R Block district mangers and staff were moved to action. One went home and signed up for a local community-service organization that connects at-risk kids with their favorite sport; another responded to a request from one of his coworkers to participate in a Big Brother program.

Still another told me afterward, "This raises the bar on what we can do for each other at work. Lisa showed us that we could and should treat our tax professionals like family. I don't think this place will ever be the same."

6. Remember Your Lost Teammates
Sometimes recognition must be delivered posthumously. Offering

appreciation of a late colleague's contributions can make an enormous difference to family and friends, helping them understand how he or she was appreciated away from home.

I learned the value of this type of recognition a few years ago when my sister-in-law, Debbie, died of a sudden aortic aneurysm. Seventy people attended her funeral, more than half of whom were her coworkers at a Citibank processing office in Las Vegas. I knew who they were because all of them dressed in tie-dyed shirts in remembrance of Debbie's love for the Grateful Dead.

Debbie's manager then spoke about the contribution she'd made every day, not only in assisting coworkers with their jobs and helping customers solve their problems, but also touching people on a personal level.

At Debbie's Citibank location, coworkers recognize each other in writing using a device called "A World of Thanks"—a simple, globe-shaped piece of paper employees fill out and sign. When people receive one, they post it in their cubicle. Debbie's cubicle was filled with such notes.

7. Encourage Your Employees to Seize Development Opportunities

Many companies offer a wide variety of training opportunities, most of which are related to skills the employee uses on the job. Training programs also provide professional-growth opportunities in areas ranging from leadership development to financial planning. Some companies offer tuition reimbursement for employees who take work-related courses at a local college; others even offer scholarships to pursue specific degrees. All of these options enable a company to add social value to its employees' lives.

If you're a manager, take note of all the opportunities that apply to your people, on the job and off. Encourage them to attend training programs; offer customized recommendations. One place to do that is in your employees' annual or quarterly performance review. At the end of the meeting, suggest a training opportunity; send a link to the program by e-mail.

You may be tempted to resist because of the scarcity mind-set (not enough time to get the work done). But when a manager stands between a corporate training program and a willing participant, a social opportunity is missed. Find a way to approve a training request, even if it means you have to scramble to cover for them.

8. Find a Miserable Job and Give It a Makeover

In his bestselling book *The Three Signs of a Miserable Job*, Patrick Lencioni quotes a recent Gallup poll finding that 70 percent of American workers hate their jobs. According to Lencioni, "The primary source of job misery and the potential cure for that misery resides in the hands of one individual—the direct manager."

Through working with thousands of Fortune 500 workers and managers, Lencioni's consulting firm, The Table Group, has discovered three conditions that create a miserable job. The first is anonymity, or "the feeling that employees get when they realize that their manager has little interest in them as a human being." The second sign is irrelevance, which takes root when employees cannot see how their job makes a difference in the lives of others. The third sign Lencioni calls "immeasurement," which is the inability of employees to assess for themselves their contribution or success.

Does the previous passage describe the day-to-day feelings of any of your employees? Are you taking personal responsibility for the quality of their work experience?

To make over a miserable job, you must first develop a sincere interest in your employees as people. Ask them about their immediate family. Do they have significant others? Kids? Pets? Can you name two non-work-related passions of each of your direct reports?

Next, give your employees a sense of their contribution to the big picture. The key is to be realistic. When I ran the ValueLab think tank at Yahoo!, my researchers toiled away collecting volumes of data that were passed on to executives and sales staff for client meetings.

To help my employees realize their contribution to the bigger picture, I developed a quarterly internal document called "The Shadow Report," which measured how much revenue was associated with my team. We tracked each sales opportunity in which ValueLab participated; when the sale closed, we entered the sales figures into a spreadsheet. At the end of each quarter, the spreadsheet calculated individual and team contributions to the company's total revenues.

For example, in the third quarter of 2002, the ValueLab helped create 10 percent of total revenues. "The Shadow Report" quickly became a source of pride for my team, helping each member understand his or her role in the company's success.

Here's another example: Most staff at pharmaceutical companies perform office functions or are tucked away in research labs, far from the patients whose health their products serve. Unlike doctors, nurses, and sales reps, these staffers lack connection with the human side of their business, and thus the value of their work.

At Abbott Labs, which makes ABT-378, a protease inhibitor used by people with AIDS, managers brought patients to headquarters and company events to share their success stories. When they told office workers and researchers how ABT-378 gave them back their lives, they gave employees a strong sense of their contributions to a real person's life.

Another aspect of the job makeover is the creation of metrics so employees can measure their successes. The key is to make the metric objective and accessible to the employee, especially during the gaps between quarterly or annual reviews.

For example, how about giving paper pushers a quality-versus-quantity metric, under which they track the number of items they process versus the number of errors they make? Customer-service workers could receive reports on their average call time (which measures cost) versus their ratio of satisfied customers (which measures quality).

In many cases, such data already exist somewhere in the company; all you need to do is request weekly or monthly reports based on call logs or incoming customer post-call surveys. Once you construct this type of metric, create a realistic goal each employee can work to meet.

9. Provide Natural Light

Many employees spend their entire work life under artificial lights. This situation can affect their moods as well as their performance. A landmark 2003 study for the Environmental Protection Agency by Rensselaer Polytechnic Institute found that natural light improves an employee's vision, function, and productivity, but most important, mood—it wards off depression and alleviates job stress.

In their book *Cradle to Cradle*, William McDonough and Michael Braungart talk about a new Herman Miller furniture factory that was redesigned with bigger windows and skylights, allowing sunshine to pour into the entire workspace. The employees' mood improved immediately, and so did productivity.

The factory managers noticed a side benefit as well: A number of workers who left for higher wages at a competitor's factory returned in a few weeks. Asked why, they told management they couldn't stand to work in the dark.

You can also make a difference with seating assignments. It's easy enough to move people around, especially in a cubicle environment, so that no employee has to work in 100 percent artificial light for more than a few months at a time.

No matter what your job title, you can effect change. At Aveda, an electrician came across a Web site featuring a new hybrid lighting system developed by Oak Ridge National Labs. Unlike solar power, which transforms sunshine into electricity, the hybrid system pulls sunlight into a rooftop dish and pipes it into the building, spraying it directly into a room while filtering out any harmful rays.

The electrician, who was working in a windowless room at the time, thought it was an excellent idea and showed it to his boss, mechanical engineer Jim Gausman. Gausman decided the system would mesh naturally with Aveda's alternative-energy program, so he pitched it to CEO Dominique Conseil, who immediately gave it the green light.

10. Limit Daily Computer Time to Five Hours or Less

An extensive 2002 study conducted by researchers at Tokyo's Chiba University determined that "mental health and sleep-related symptoms were significantly higher in the group [of workers] having more than five hours of daily computer use."

When the results were published in the *American Journal of Industrial Medicine*, the editors pointed out that once that five-hour threshold was crossed, the dangers "of psychological disorders setting in appeared to increase sharply."

This observation was particularly true when workers weren't given regular computer breaks. In 2003, I partnered with Heartmath Institute, a leading researcher in occupational health and safety, to test the validity of the Chiba University study. After surveying 3,000 diverse information workers, we also discovered a statistically significant relationship between the amount of time one spends at a computer and depression symptoms, the effects of which can lead to heart disease, high blood pressure, and a weakened immune system. Follow-up phone interviews with several respondents by psychotherapist Terrance Real confirmed this link.

Yet, according to the technology-research firm Metafacts, approximately 5 million workers spend more than eight hours a day looking at computer screens. Metafacts' research also indicates that an additional 7 million workers must log in five to six hours of screen time daily.

Instead of chaining employees to computers for long stretches, chop up the workday. Help people take a break from their computers at least once an hour. Never let them work at a computer station more than three hours in a row. The Chiba University study found that frequent breaks significantly reduced the risk of depression.

Allow for non-screen-time activities, including face-to-face meetings, conference calls, and reading trade journals and books. When you infuse a computer-based job with three hours a day of social and educational activities, you raise the quality of work life and reduce the damage done by computer overuse. You're also abiding by the Law of the Ledger; a 2003 study by the *Journal of the American Medical Association* estimated that $44 billion in productivity is lost each year due to work-related depression.

11. Promote Workplace Wellness Programs

Wellness programs promote healthy living and are aimed at preventing illness. These programs can include free flu shots, education programs, workout facilities, diet consultations, and smoking-cessation programs.

If your employer offers a wellness program, sign up to participate. Studies at office-furniture maker Steelcase Inc. and Pepsi Bottling found that such programs can dramatically decrease your chances of coming down with a serious illness due to lifestyle or diet, reducing your annual sick days and increasing your productivity.

Your participation in a wellness program will also set an example for your coworkers and help build a healthy culture at work. The directors of wellness programs I interviewed all agreed that wide participation signals to corporate that wellness is a popular and sound investment, which in turn helps to ensure such programs will be sustained and expanded.

But don't just sign up—take time to learn about the program's different elements and talk about the options with your coworkers. If you're a manager, make wellness programs a group endeavor. Instead of positioning the program as corporate, make it employee-based. According to David Kasiarz, vice president of compensation benefits and risk management at Pepsi Bottling, that clarification will dramatically increase participation by your group.

Tie wellness to goodness. A group of employees at Pepsi Bottling's Knoxville location created a campus promotion in which they encouraged fitness through a Habitat for Humanity program. Dozens of employees worked up a sweat as they swung hammers and wielded saws to build homes. Along the way, the effort generated positive television coverage for the company.

If you don't have a wellness program at your company, meet with your boss and advocate for one, as did Diane Ball, a cardiac rehab nurse at Illinois' Delnor Community Hospital.

In 1999, Ball attended a stress-reduction seminar conducted by Heartmath on behalf of her patients, who needed to manage stress to recover fully from cardiac illnesses. But she realized it was helping her, too.

At the time, the environment at Delnor was very intense; Ball's coworkers needed stress management as badly as recovering heart attack patients did. Because Ball had no authority and no direct reports, she approached her boss, a hospital vice president, and said that although she was considering leaving, she'd stay if he allowed her to bring Heartmath into Delnor.

Impressed, Ball's boss brought the issue to Tom Wright, the hospital's chief operating officer, and convinced him to fly to Heartmath's headquarters in California to attend a stress-management workshop. After attending, Wright realized that the program was exactly what Delnor needed to improve productivity and reduce staff turnover, which at the time was 28 percent, much higher than the national average.

The program, launched in 2001, led to a rapid change in the quality of life and services at the hospital; turnover fell by half. According to data compiled by the management consulting firm Sperduto, from 2002 to 2006 Delnor was rated number one nationally in the annual rankings in its category for employee satisfaction. The hospital was also honored three years in a row by the state of Illinois' annual Companies That Care awards.

12. Don't Encroach on Personal or Family Time

Because the current business edict seems to be that we should accomplish more work with fewer people, for many employees, the Monday-through-Friday workweek has morphed into the Monday-through-Sunday treadmill. Bad idea! Weekends or holidays are not extra innings that managers can use to grab more time from salaried employees.

Similarly, corporate events or meetings should not be scheduled during employee personal time. The trend has been to schedule sales conferences and off-site meetings for weekends or holidays so they don't "interfere with normal work." Compelled to attend, employees lose valuable family time as well as much-needed breaks to recover from the week.

If your meeting isn't important enough to take time off from office work during the week, why have it in the first place? Stand up for your employees' weekends by scheduling meetings during normal business hours.

Make it a general rule, as SAS Institute does, to force even the workaholics to "go home and be with your family and friends." Fast-food enterprise Chick-Fil-A believes this credo so strongly that more than two decades ago it made the decision to close the company every Sunday, as its research told them that Sunday was the best day for employees to connect with loved ones as well as to worship or rest.

13. Demand the Highest Levels of Safety for Employees

Social innovators have a zero-tolerance policy for worker injuries; companies from Patagonia to Aveda make worker safety a sacrosanct principle. You should, too.

If you don't work at a factory, you may think that your company creates few injuries. But many office employees suffer from back-related issues as well as carpal tunnel syndrome stemming from hours at the computer. Do your knowledge workers receive adequate wrist and back support? Are they given ergonomic equipment? Are your customer-service representatives bearing the emotional brunt of your company's setbacks in service or product quality? Are your frequent travelers risking their health by flying hundreds of thousands of miles a year?

Any damage incurred by your employees, emotional or physical, can be a source of liability for companies. Addressing the issue is good for both employees and the company over the long haul.

By demanding this highest level of job safety, you create a culture of protection as opposed to a culture of compliance, or as Ray Anderson calls the practice, "being as bad as the law will allow."

14. Champion Diversity

During the upcoming war for talent, top candidates will use diversity as a tiebreaker when deciding between companies; they see it as a matter of good management that social innovators hire, accept, and respect employees from diverse backgrounds.

Support diversity through your own hiring practices; assess your group or division as well. As you review applications for open positions, consider a candidate's contribution to your group's diversity in addition to their on-paper qualifications.

Consider your words, too. Diversity champions use inclusive language. For example, when referring to leaders, don't always use the pronoun "he," or when planning an event that includes significant others, don't say "bring your husbands or wives"; say "bring your partner."

You can also communicate respect and acceptance for diversity by supporting diversity groups inside your company. Typically called affinity groups, employee resource groups, or stakeholder alliances, such teams include employees who represent a specific minority population at the company and who advocate for inclusion and equality.

Diversity of thought will most likely arise from a diversity of people. In 2005, Columbia Business School professor Elizabeth Mannix and Stanford Business School professor Margaret Neale, who conducted a multiyear study of diversity's impact on innovation, noted: "Diversity is especially important and beneficial for problem solving and innovation tasks."

The authors pointed out that leading tech companies such as Google, Hewlett-Packard, Microsoft, and IBM have long employed diverse cultures in their R&D departments. They are also top innovators in their categories.

Partners

Few businesses can manage successfully without business partners. Partners help a company do everything your company can't do alone:

They ship your packages, clean your office, market your products, file your taxes, and so on.

Partners must be given the same respect that a company extends to its employees. Too often we try to squeeze value out of them: Distributors get commissions slashed without notice, accountants are fired for no stated reason, suppliers are expected to be subservient to customers' whims.

In almost every industry, there are too many suppliers with too few buyers, a lack of balance that gives power to the buyer. With this power comes a sense of entitlement that suppliers should do whatever the customer wishes, allowing buyers to feel they can dictate absolute terms.

This strategy will backfire during the Responsibility Revolution. The way a company treats its business partners is a key driver of its social reputation, according to the Golin-Harris 2006 research. Get it wrong and your company's reputation will suffer: In the view of the business community and the public, a company's treatment of its partners is an undeniable test of its ethics.

Take Wal-Mart. Even though the company has recently adopted innovative environmental practices and designed a better health care package for its employees, its reputation for strong-arming its suppliers irks the business community and spills over into the general public's view of the company's ethics.

When you improve your relations with your partners, you boost your brand and upgrade the reputation of your business operations. This fact is one of the secrets to membership-based discount retailer Costco's success. CEO Jim Sinegal, who founded the company in 1993, has built a culture committed to delivering customers low prices and showing all partners dignity and respect.

While working at Yahoo!, I asked Sinegal about Costco's vendor policies and supplier codes. He quickly corrected me: "We call them partners. We rely on them to stock our shelves, delight our shoppers, and help us run our business."

Costco's investment in partner relations has convinced exclusive electronics brands such as Sony, which normally doesn't sell its products in a warehouse setting, to do so, giving shoppers an opportunity to save money on items never before available in a discount environment. This practice also helps explain why Costco outsells Sam's Club (a discounter owned by Wal-Mart) despite the fact that it has two hundred fewer stores. According to *Fortune* magazine, the company is one of the most admired in America, with employee and supplier relations contributing heavily to its ranking.

When companies invest in supplier relationships, quality and selection improve, which in turn affects the customer experience positively. Daniel Barry, an analyst with Merrill Lynch, told *Fortune*, "Costco is relentless in its mission to have a treasure-hunt feel, to create a place that's exciting to shop."

You can build this kind of culture too, one partner at a time, by following these pieces of advice:

1. Treat All Partners as Equals

As seventeenth-century Japanese traders traveled to neighboring countries, they experienced cultural conflicts with their trading partners. So trader Soan Suminokura partnered with Confucian scholar Seika Fujiwara to develop a practice called *Shuchu Kiyaku*, a code of ethics designed to avoid conflict while building successful long-term relationships. It involved two rules. Rule One: The trade must benefit both parties. Rule Two: All partners should be treated as equals regardless of economic or cultural status.

Although the practice eventually withered, Japanese companies such as Canon and Nissan resurrected this style of trading during the Quality Revolution in the 1980s and 1990s, teaching their internal buyers how to listen to, respect, and mentor partners. These companies shared relevant data with suppliers and distributors as if these people were a part of the company.

This expression of trust created a sense of egalitarianism between the company and its partner that improved not only performance but relationships as well. To this day, Nissan has a far better reputation among suppliers than its American counterparts GM and Ford (as measured by the "Working Relations" study conducted annually by automotive researcher Planned Perspectives).

2. Support Your Partners' Business

Too often we batter partners to achieve the best possible prices or terms, then wonder why they seem to struggle financially.

Support your partners' businesses by paying a reasonable price or standard commissions. Bargaining for the short term has to be reconciled with the impact it will have on your partners' long-term loyalty. You'll be less likely to have to change partners, and more likely to get a break when you need one.

Pay your partners quickly. Many companies drag their feet, or create hurdles when paying their suppliers, distributors, and/or contractors; this practice is especially common at large companies and government agencies. Why create cash-flow problems for your vendor? It's hardly a prescription for their long-term success. Be your partner's in-house advocate: Motivate your finance folks to expedite payment.

And be considerate when it comes to your partners' expenses. Too often they're forced to process unnecessary paperwork and redo work that is acceptable. Avoid creating wasteful activities— the best companies equate wasting their partner's money with wasting their own.

3. Think Loyal

The Law of the Long View says if you commit to your partners, you're committed for the long haul. It's your job to stick with them even if a short-term reason to change arises.

Too often we treat partners with a what-have-you-done-for-me-lately attitude, or a lowest-price-wins-my-business mind-set. Such thinking can result in product recalls, disappointed customers, and damage to the company brand.

For example, with its cheap labor, China can often underprice an American competitor, but unlike their Japanese counterparts in decades past, Chinese manufacturers are not accomplishing this feat with quality improvement. Quite the opposite. In 2007, millions of inexpensively made Chinese products, from pet food to toys, were recalled from store shelves due to their low quality and harmful ingredients. Mattel, Sony, Dell, and a host of pet-food companies have paid a penalty for working with such low-cost partners.

On the other hand, ice-cream maker Ben & Jerry's cofounder Ben Cohen is committed to buying his milk from local dairy farmers. He believes that local farms are critical to sustainable agriculture, a belief codified in the company's social-responsibility program.

Ben & Jerry's loyalty was challenged in the late 1980s when industrial-sized farms, often owned by multinational companies, began offering lower wholesale milk prices. Cohen believed such pricing, driven by technological advances, was only a temporary cost advantage. So, remaining loyal to local dairy farmers, he actively helped them catch up with their larger competitors by, among other things, launching an ambitious set of educational programs to aid local farmers in bridging the knowledge/tech gap.

Working with the local farms cost the company a great deal of money in the short run. But it paid off in the long run—the Ben & Jerry's strategy helped the company offer high-quality products and

lower average costs by maintaining consistent relationships throughout its supply chain—all because Ben & Jerry's kept its promises.

4. Mentor Your Partners

One of the greatest value-adds you can share with your partners is
knowledge.

Equal Exchange is a retailer of coffee to restaurants across the
United States. Due to quality issues, the retail coffee industry rejects
a high percentage of coffee beans from smaller producers, often because the farmers who grow them haven't been taught how to raise
beans that sell well to Western companies.

In response, Equal Exchange mentors its farmers, most of whom
reside in Central and South America, on state-of-the-art growing
and processing methods that enable them to improve their coffee-
bean quality. In addition to offering field training, the company pays
for farmers to visit its Massachusetts headquarters.

Both programs have reduced coffee-bean rejection rates and
boosted labor productivity. In 2006, one Nicaraguan farmer, Arnaldo Neyra Camizan, told a *Fast Company* reporter, "Through Equal
Exchange's help, our members are converting from small-scale
farmers to small-scale businesspeople."

Organize an educational event for partners. First, survey both
the partner and your colleagues to determine what knowledge would
add the most value. Next, create a curriculum (including best practices presentations). Allot time for questions and answers. Follow
up the meeting with a summary of the best ideas from the event.
Measure the results over time so you can calculate the financial return on your investment.

Another approach is to provide one-on-one mentoring. If you
work with a partner whose success is dependent on more knowledge,
make him or her your personal project. Talk to colleagues and staff

members about how they can mentor outside contacts who could use their help. If you're a manager, include these mentorship efforts in employees' annual reviews and reward them for success.

The beauty of mentorship is that you create a positive feedback loop in which your partners share knowledge with you as well. This is a natural result of the Law of Reciprocity: When you give, others give back.

5. Share Your Network

Your partners almost always need more contacts. Some of them may be in start-up phase and seek more customers, capital, and/or partners. But mature companies, too, need a constant infusion of new contacts to help keep them on the cutting edge.

You can help by hosting networking events. Such events are a low-cost means of dramatically improving partner relations, as well as improving your reputation as a partner.

A wide variety of companies, including consumer products maker Unilever and technology provider Cisco Networks, employ such events as part of their partner-development programs. The format is simple: Invite companies relevant to a specific set of partners and create a structured conversation around a relevant topic. Networking events do best when accompanied by a promise of valuable content as well as new contacts that can result in new partnerships.

You can also bring partners together in a smaller setting, such as a lunch, as did a highly successful New York City insurance salesman in the 1930s. For more than a decade, Elmer Letterman hosted networking lunches every Friday at the Four Seasons restaurant. His strategy was simple: invite three businesspeople who should meet due to mutual interests. He did his homework, too, arriving with ideas on how the three could work together.

For example, Letterman might invite a chef who wanted to start a restaurant, a banker who could finance it, and a construction executive who could build it. He'd explain why each party was credible and relevant to the others, begin a conversation, pay the bill, and leave.

How did these networking investments pay off? Do the math: three people times fifty weeks a year, for a decade. Hundreds of business owners throughout New York had Letterman to thank for part of their success. According to Ivan Misner's book *Masters of Networking*, Letterman not only developed a reputation as a major contributor to New York's business community, he was one of the most successful insurance business owners of his time.

Today, you can network partners via conference calls as well. Make an introduction through a three-way e-mail. Introduce each party in the body of the e-mail and spell out why you think they should get to know one another. Invite them to contact one another directly and, if possible, to meet. Don't focus on your own interest; the key here is to think of networking as a gift, not a tool to extract lower prices or favorable terms down the line.

Such gifts don't have to be purely professional; you can also help out on a personal level. Devin Poulter, a salesperson at software reseller Software Spectrum, did just that, as I found out when I spoke at his company's sales conference in 2004. Afterward, a handful of reps approached me to talk about Devin, their in-house hero. When I tracked him down, he agreed to tell me the story of how he'd earned that reputation.

One of Devin's roles was to manage relationships with the software companies that supplied the company with its products. One day, he was on a routine phone call with a supplier named Mary. Sensing she was sad, Devin asked, "You sound like you're having a terrible day. Would you like to talk about it?"

She declined, but a few minutes later blurted out, "Well, you've really opened up a can of worms here." Mary proceeded to explain how she and her husband had been trying to adopt a baby from Russia and had faced a series of seemingly insurmountable obstacles along the way. They were ready to give up. Devin commiserated, then launched into action.

Earlier, he'd worked with a woman named Maureen who had successfully adopted a Russian baby, so he decided to introduce her to Mary via e-mail. Maureen in turn invited Mary to join a support group for other families in a similar situation. Buoyed by the support group and their newfound knowledge, Mary and her husband pursued their quest; eight months later, they adopted a girl. Mary sent Devin a picture of the baby with this note: "This is the fruit of our labors. Thank you for everything you've done for us."

Although Devin didn't discuss his good deed, his workmates at Software Spectrum did, and the story greatly shapes the company's reputation.

6. Be Willing to Forgive

Face it. Partners make mistakes. They may have lapses in service or glitches in product quality. When this happens, respond with compassion rather than vengefulness.

Certainly, chronically underperforming partners must be replaced. But don't adopt a one-mistake-kills-the-relationship business style.

For more than a decade, Cummins Diesel Inc., a producer of engines and related technologies, has maintained a Supplier Coaching Program centered on Six Sigma quality-assurance training. (Six Sigma is a manufacturing-management process, pioneered at Motorola during the Quality Revolution, that all but eliminates product defects.)

The company knows suppliers make mistakes, often because of a lack of training or supply-chain information. But Cummins' leaders also realize that if they summarily fired every supplier who wasn't perfect, they'd spend all their time searching for new ones.

Their motto is: Retrain, don't fire. Based on its reputation for good supplier relations (as well as its work on clean diesel technology), Cummins has appeared on the *Business Ethics* Corporate Citizen Top 100 list every year since it was started in 1999; in 2005, it placed first.

Equal Exchange, the coffee distributor, shares the same philosophy but takes a different approach. Because the company buys from small farmers in developing nations, coffee-bean quality varies. This is not acceptable to the restaurants and coffeehouses to whom Equal Exchange sells. The company issues quality standards to farmers, and in many cases these standards aren't met.

However, unlike their competitors, who would simply abrogate the contracts at this point, Equal Exchange first cuts the bean order by 20 percent to send a message about its commitment to quality standards. In addition, it offers training to help its partner achieve acceptable levels of quality. Then, in most cases, the farmer works his or her way back to acceptable quality standards, at which point Equal Exchange restores 100 percent of its business.

7. Support Equal Opportunity

Thousands of small businesses owned by women or members of minority groups struggle to compete against much larger and better-connected rivals. Discrimination exists. It's up to you as a saver soldier to seek out strong partners who could benefit from equal opportunity.

For retail stores, vendors are key partners—they provide the products the stores sell. Office Depot, a leader in vendor diversity, uses a program designed to help HUBs (historically underutilized businesses) win vendor contracts by teaching them how to be more competitive and land their products on store shelves next to major brands.

HUBs typically lack marketing and advertising dollars, so purchasing agents at Office Depot comb trade shows looking for partner candidates. In this way, as part of the HUB search process, Office Depot, which works with the National Minority Supplier Development Council and the Women's Business Enterprise National Council, has discovered dozens of small companies eager to provide Office Depot's customers with high-quality products.

Master Manufacturing, an inner-city Cleveland-based maker of replacement casters for office chairs, is a case in point. Master is owned and operated by Iris Rubinfield, who founded the company with her husband in 1951. A longtime supporter of equal opportunity for workers, Rubinfield has provided many long-term jobs to historically underemployed groups; some 90 percent of her employees are women or members of minority groups.

Office Depot features Master's products, along with its story, in its mail-order catalog as well as on its shelves. This free promotion has helped the company become the country's top producer of replacement casters, enabling it to expand its product line to include ergonomic office-chair parts, cushions, and rubber door stoppers.

The program is also a winner for Office Depot, providing access to hard-to-find, high-quality products while helping differentiate the company from its competitors in the minds of consumers.

8. Champion Off-Site Workers

Your off-site contract workers are your partners, too, and deserve as much consideration. Aveda's CEO, Dominique Conseil, has a standard question whenever he's presented with a new beauty or personal-care product: "How did you do that?" He wants an accounting of the labor and materials that went into the item's production.

If you don't ask about your partners' working conditions, you'll never know—unless the media or a watchdog group tells you first. In 1995, the National Labor Committee, a sweatshop watchdog group, released a report based on an investigation of television personality Kathie Lee Gifford's line of clothes, which she produced for Wal-Mart. The report documented that one out of ten workers in her Honduras plant were twelve to fourteen years old and often forced to work twelve-hour shifts without any breaks. The report also revealed that Gifford was using sweatshop labor in Manhattan, paying sixty cents per hour while requiring ten- to eleven-hour shifts. Many of the Manhattan workers reported being unpaid for months.

Wal-Mart received thousands of calls and letters from angry shoppers and activists in response to the report. College students staged protests inside Wal-Mart stores carrying Gifford's line and then handed out flyers in the parking lots, garnering national publicity. ABC, the network that produced *Live with Regis and Kathie Lee*, went on the offensive to restore her reputation.

Shedding tears on television, Gifford proclaimed her ignorance of the situation and promised to donate 10 percent of her future profits to children's charities. Meanwhile, her husband, sports commentator Frank Gifford, went to the Manhattan factory and handed out hundred-dollar bills to workers.

Despite the attempts to repair her image, sales of Kathie Lee's clothing never regained their pre-1995 levels. (For its part, Wal-Mart publicly denounced sweatshop labor and promised to step up its inspections of labor conditions at factories that made the products it carried.)

Ask your partners questions about products, services, or processes that involve outsourced work. Request that your partners trace the labor behind their services and provide an accounting for wage and working conditions. If your suppliers don't know their sources, give them a reasonable but firm period of time in which to provide you with an accounting.

Make this policy a part of your contract with suppliers, giving your company the right to audit working conditions for contract labor and, if unsatisfied, to cancel the contract. This stipulation will put teeth in your commitment to protect all workers.

9. Meet Your Global Partners

If your company works with partners in other countries, boost your relationships by visiting them in their working environment. If you've never met them, how can you show them the same compassion shown your workers at headquarters? After all, you depend on these people for success.

Global partners include any business that performs an activity your company wants to outsource, such as call centers that provide customer support, the farmers or factories that tend to your resources, technology companies that help manage your Web sites, and so on.

Bob Stiller is the founder and CEO of Vermont's Green Mountain Coffee Roasters, a specialty producer of organic and Fair Trade Certified coffee. In 1991, Stiller started sending employees to La Minita Tarrazu in Costa Rica, asking them to talk to the growers to learn how coffee travels from the tree to the cup.

According to Michael Dupee, the company's vice president of corporate social responsibility, the human connection transforms the visitors. When they return, employees then share their experiences back at headquarters, showing pictures and telling stories about the farmers and their families.

Twenty percent of all employees at Green Mountain have now visited a coffee farm in Central or South America. These "trips to source," as Green Mountain calls them, have improved partner relations as well as enhanced the company's reputation: In 2006, *Business Ethics* magazine ranked Green Mountain as the best corporate citizen in the United States.

If your company works with global partners, find out whether a program exists to facilitate on-site employee visits. Such programs are usually located in the procurement, purchasing, or human resources department. If you're a manager and some of your staff work with global partners, nominate one of them to visit the source. If no program exists, suggest that one be created. And why not offer to go on the first trip?

10. Whenever Possible, Purchase Products That Are Certified as Fair Trade

Fair trade is a movement among suppliers, producers, retailers, and consumers to guarantee that producers in developing countries are fairly compensated and social and environmental standards are enforced. In this way, the movement seeks to rectify the vulnerable position of small-scale producers when dealing with multinational companies.

Historically, fair-trade discussions have centered on coffee producers. But fair trade is not just for breakfast anymore. Any labor-intensive business in a developing country is eligible for fair-trade certification or investigation. Products in question can include coffee, tea, cocoa, chocolate, fruit, cotton, wine, and diamonds.

If one of those products is served or produced anywhere within your corporate facility, find out if they are Fair Trade Certified, a mark authenticated by a company called TransFair USA.

Anyone can make a difference—in and out of the workplace. In

2001, five student members of the UCLA Environmental Coalition drafted a document advocating that Fair Trade Certified coffee be served in school cafeterias. Group leaders presented their case in a meeting with the dining services department and school administrators. Moved by the student's arguments, the dining services department went to its supplier, Sara Lee Corporation, and requested Fair Trade Certified coffee.

According to Nick Obourn, editor for *Fresh Cup*, a fair-trade industry publication, "The victory was influential for many reasons: It changed the viewpoint of one of the largest coffee distributors in the United States; it was the impetus for Sara Lee to supply Fair Trade Certified coffee to other accounts, including 250 Borders Bookstores; and for many it marked the beginning of the fair-trade movement on campuses."

You can also ask hotels and conference centers to use Fair Trade Certified products at your corporate events. Most hotels will provide precisely the products you request. If enough companies ask enough venues to change, Fair Trade Certified alternatives could be featured at events across the nation.

Remember, markets are conversations, so start a good one!

11

Act: Save Your Communities

Community-relations development is the process of forging a bond between your company and the community in which it does business. Your company is either a nutrient, a filler, or a toxin to its communities.

Community relations count for a significant portion of a company's social status. The Golin-Harris survey ranks being "active and involved in communities where it does business" as a primary driver in a company's standing as a good corporate citizen.

A company's reputation as an employer of choice is also at stake: The Work Foundation survey mentioned earlier noted that one out of three ThemGeners said they were planning to find a new job because their employer's community contributions were subpar.

Companies should become involved in host communities due, in part, to the Law of Reciprocity. After all, communities often give financial incentives, such as tax breaks, to companies. They also supply employees, local customers, professional services, school systems for children, sewage, garbage disposal, and even security (the police force).

The secret to being effective in community outreach is a high level of employee participation, as evidenced by the success of Timberland. As mentioned earlier, Timberland's sales reps gave away their shoes in New Orleans, but their familiarity with community service runs much deeper vis-à-vis a relationship with City Year, a division of America Corps, in which young adults volunteer to serve local communities for one year.

In 1989, City Year officials asked Timberland for fifty pairs of work boots for a local project in Boston. Intrigued with the program, the company's CEO, Jeffrey Swartz, approved the donation. When Alan Khazei, one of the project's founders, went to Timberland headquarters to thank Swartz, a strategic partnership was formed.

A 1996 Harvard Business School case study captured the exchange between the two that day: Swartz says, "When Alan came by to say thanks for the boots, I said to him, 'You are doing the things with your life that I dream about doing with mine. You are out there actually saving lives. I am making boots, but I have always wanted to save lives.'"

Khazei added, "Let me show you how they can be related . . . I will provide you with a vehicle for your beliefs."

A few weeks later, Swartz made a $50,000 cash donation to City Year.

While Khazei appreciated the cash, what he really wanted from Timberland was people power. He got it after Swartz himself volunteered for a local project. Because he did, he better understood the value of the program to his company, and in 1992 he created Path of Service, a program that gave employees up to fifteen hours a year of time off to work on City Year projects in their local communities. Over the next few years, Timberland employees joined City Year projects all along the northeastern United States. In 1997, Swartz expanded the program to forty hours of paid community service a year and even created a handful of yearlong employee sabbaticals.

Then, in 2003, Timberland and City Year launched the Community Builders Tour, fanning out nationwide and partnering with local residents and retailers to take on larger local projects such as re-building schools, playgrounds, and community centers. City Year received press coverage, local communities got donated labor, and everybody involved in the project wore Timberland apparel, giving the company free advertising.

In less than two decades, Timberland employees have contributed more than 250,000 hours of time in more than two hundred communities. Moreover, Timberland has developed a national reputation for being an excellent employer, appearing on every one of *Fortune*'s Best Companies to Work For lists since the list's inception. The company's involvement with City Year has been recognized by three American presidents as well as more than a dozen nonprofits that measure socially responsible business practices.

Internal surveys at Timberland revealed that the Path of Service program has been one of two top sources of employee job satisfaction. For recruiters, the program is one of the most important perks they discuss when trying to attract potential employees.

Timberland eventually took the concept of partnership with City Year to its logical extreme: The two organizations integrated. Today, they share offices in Boston as well as human resources departments. Timberland provides people power, money, and advice to City Year, which in return appears at employee and shareholder meetings to share success stories about the partnership.

Most important, 90 percent of Timberland employees participate in Path of Service, donating forty hours a year to work in communities while on the clock.

Every one of you can help your company serve the communities in which it does business. Almost all businesses have community outreach programs that encourage employee participation. For those involved in these projects, your contributions will be evaluated by the strength of your efforts and ideas rather than your role or rank.

1. Join an Existing Community Program

The assessment you completed in Chapter 9 may have turned up information on your company's involvement in the local community. You can also log on to the company intranet, look under Community Affairs or Public Relations, and find a list of all its community programs. Or just call your community affairs department or talk to your manager. (If your company is small, ask around—perhaps your president, or even a coworker, knows of programs in which your company is involved.)

Find a program that excites you. Does it match your personal values? Is it consistent with your lifestyle? Look for something that can intelligently incorporate your skills. Liking a program is important, but finding one in which you can really make a difference is more so. Search out opportunities that leverage your education or experience as well as your network.

Next, check to see if the program is connected in some way to the company's business. Does it reflect your company's values? This will make the program credible to your coworkers, as it represents a natural extension of the business rather than being simply your personal cause.

Is there a long-term benefit for the company? If so, it will help you avoid investing time in a program that may be terminated if business conditions worsen. A program with a powerful connection to your business is one with a future.

Give priority to programs that allow participants time off. Many companies offer sabbaticals of up to a year for community service. Such a sabbatical can provide you with a life-changing experience and a new set of skills.

When signing up for such a program, make a professional commitment to it, such as a minimum one-year pledge with clearly stated goals. Track it in your Day-Timer or online calendar, just as you track your progress in work-related projects.

If you manage employees, encourage them to become involved in a community program, too. Because such contributions are good for the business in the long run, include the involvement in your reviews when you sum up your employees' job performance.

2. Create a Virtuous Circle in Your Community

If you can't find a program that suits your and your company's needs, consider creating your own. Try to produce a virtuous circle, in which the company addresses a community issue in a way that connects it to the success of the business; the more that you invest into your community, the more the community will patronize your business.

In the section on the Law of Interdependence, I talked about how UPS simultaneously addressed Louisville's high school graduation-rate decline while solving its staffing issues. Another example: Cisco, producer of information technology equipment.

Cisco realized back in the mid-1990s that a worldwide shortage of information technology (IT) professionals would arise around the year 2004, limiting the growth of Cisco's networking business. So, in 1997, the company launched the Cisco Networking Academy, a program focusing on economically challenged neighborhoods in seven states. Cisco donated computers to schools and provided students with instructions in network administration and computer sciences.

A few years later, the program was expanded overseas, and today more than 1.6 million students in 10,000 academies around the world have been trained for the IT business.

You don't have to work at a multinational to accomplish similar goals. Los Angeles law firm Munger, Tolles & Olson supports a community-based program that promotes public speaking and debate skills. Partners at the firm donate time, money, and expertise to help kids in the most challenged urban neighborhoods learn how to debate. (Research shows that kids with debating skills triple their chance of attending college.)

At a networking luncheon hosted by the firm on behalf of the debate league, one of the firm's senior partners said, "By investing in this program . . . we're going to create an endless supply of great legal minds from some of the most underprivileged communities in Los Angeles."

If this strategy makes sense, look for problems in the communities in which your company does business; search for a match between the problem and your company's resources and expertise.

Next, develop a business case for action. See if you can create a virtuous circle, like Cisco's, to ensure that your program will be sustainable even if economic conditions worsen. As Harvard Business School professor Michael Porter says, the acid test of a strategic corporate social-responsibility program is whether "the desired social change is so beneficial to the company that the organization would pursue the change even if no one ever knew about it."

Bryan Sperber, the president of the Phoenix International Raceway, created such a virtuous circle. The local host for NASCAR races, Sperber attended one of my lectures, went home, did some research, and discovered that car accidents were the chief cause of death for Arizona high school students. He decided kids needed better defensive-driving programs as well as more access to experts. "By leveraging our expertise," he told me, "we want to take defensive-driving programs to high schools as well as Arizona State University. Our goal is to sharpen the defensive-driving skills of people ages fifteen to twenty-one."

Using professional drivers makes defensive-driving instruction sexy. And, because Sperber's defensive-driving program is now part of high school and college curricula, he's introducing a new generation of young drivers to the concept of attending the racetrack.

3. Sponsor Community Organizations

Whether you work at a large or a small company, explore possible local sponsorship opportunities.

FedEx did just that in 2000 when the company launched its Walk This Way program in partnership with Safe Kids Worldwide, an educational program designed to reduce pedestrian injuries among children. The connection: FedEx is recognized as a leader in safety, both in its driving record and its work operations (one of its long-standing corporate credos is "Safety Above All").

The company's CEO, David Bronczek, says, "There is nothing more fearful for a FedEx courier than a child darting out in front of your truck. Safe Kids Worldwide is a perfect fit for us."

Pedestrian injuries are the second-leading cause of accidental death for five- to fourteen-year-olds. Since 2000, thousands of FedEx employees have sponsored Safe Kids by providing their safety expertise, volunteering to help during the International Walk to School Day every October, and staffing local task forces in high-risk areas.

FedEx's involvement has helped Walk This Way prosper and expand to Canada, Brazil, China, South Korea, and the Philippines. In turn, the worldwide couriers have innovated the safety program. In China, for example, drivers came up with the idea of letting children briefly sit in the truck's driver's seat so they can see exactly what the drivers see and understand the blind spots in a truck driver's vision. The idea was adopted at FedEx headquarters and is now a worldwide practice.

See if your company has such a policy on cash donations. Or call your chamber of commerce. Ask around your house of worship or at civic groups. Once you find a worthwhile project, draw up a short proposal outlining what your company would be required to contribute, your potential role, roles for other employees, how your community would benefit, how your company would benefit, and why you think it would be a good fit for all. Send this proposal to your public relations, community affairs, sales promotions, and marketing departments, or even your corporate foundation.

4. Respond to Community Crisis

Jessica Lewis, a comanager at the Waveland, Mississippi, Wal-Mart, did exactly that. On the night of August 29, 2005, when Hurricane Katrina hit, Lewis visited her store and found it flooded, its aisles ransacked and large appliances scattered around the floors.

Outside on Highway 90, she witnessed another disturbing scene: men, women, and children wandering around in their pajamas or underwear because they had no time to dress; some of them were bloody, many were crying. "It broke my heart to see them like this," Lewis told a *Fortune* reporter in October 2005. "They were the parents of the kids on my kids' sports teams. They're my neighbors. They're my customers."

Lewis asked her stepbrother, who owned a bulldozer, to clear a path through the devastated store so she could find salvageable products to hand out. She grabbed shoes, diapers, bottled water, crackers, and sausages, and even broke into the pharmacy to locate insulin for diabetics needing their prescriptions filled. She recalls telling her coworkers the next day that she hoped she wouldn't land in trouble, because she hadn't found the time to clear her response with corporate headquarters.

Her story, as well as those of other courageous Wal-Mart employees, bubbled up to the company's top brass. Two months later, Wal-Mart CEO Lee Scott gave a speech broadcast worldwide to Wal-Mart offices. He said, "When Katrina hit last month, the world saw pictures of great suffering and misery. . . . I saw the pain, the difficulty, and the tears. But I saw something else. . . . I saw how [Jessica Lewis] worked to help those in her community. Jessica Lewis didn't call the home office and ask permission. She just did the right thing."

In the minds of many local communities affected by Katrina, Wal-Mart made a bigger difference than the federal government. Dozens of store managers passed out products to needy families, and truckers hauled in $3 million worth of supplies, arriving days before the Federal Emergency Management Agency showed up.

When a crisis comes to your town, don't wait for somebody else to spring into action. Be a Jessica Lewis. Do the right thing. Make your boss happy. Make the world happy.

5. Offer Your Company as a Meeting Place
When I was growing up in Clovis, New Mexico, a popular local steakhouse called La Villa always offered its restaurant banquet room at no extra charge to community groups such as the Rotary Club and the Junior League. La Villa provided these groups with a well-stocked and -staffed venue for their meetings and created a good reputation for La Villa by association. It also introduced new customers to La Villa's fare, helping it compete with its rival, Sizzler, a national chain with more ad dollars to spend.

What if your company doesn't own a restaurant? Your boardrooms, lunchrooms, and meeting spaces can provide great opportunities for community organizations to get together, while enhancing your company's reputation as a community partner.

If your company possesses the appropriate space, see if your facilities management allows for this type of use. If your company is small, offer a local organization a chance to meet at your facility outside of company office hours. Keep your ears open for groups looking for meeting spaces, or be proactive by posting a listing on Craigslist.org.

If you have influence over your company's Web site, announce that your facility is available there. For years, the Bakersfield, California–based office supply company A. B. Dick/IPS has done just that, offering its conference room as a free meeting place for local nonprofits.

6. Lend Your Resources to a Community Organization

Salesforce.com, a provider of sales-planning software, has a community giveback program, called The One Percent Solution, in which the company gives away 1 percent of its sales in the form of product donations to nonprofit groups. Mark Benioff, company founder and Saver CEO, believes this gift is more valuable to nonprofits than a cash donation because his company's software helps them improve how they raise money and run their day-to-day operations.

Starting in 2002, Consorta, a group purchasing company that buys supplies on behalf of hospitals, lent its purchasing expertise to United Way—a good fit for Consorta because United Way has a presence in all of the cities where Consorta does business. Consorta CEO John Strong says that, by sharing its expertise with United Way, the company was able to help the organization save $7 million in the first year alone—significantly more money than Consorta could have handed directly to the nonprofit.

Giving away intangibles such as knowledge or software creates a mutual victory for company and community. Ask yourself what knowledge or technology you could give a community organization. Also, what kind of helpful advice could you receive from that organization via the feedback loop?

In the case of Salesforce.com, the nonprofits used the donated software in novel ways, then gave candid feedback to the company about how it could better tailor the product to serve fund-raising programs. This feedback helped Salesforce.com improve its software and expand its potential market to serve associations, membership-driven groups, and the rest of the social sector.

7. Buy Local

How you spend your company's money matters to the local communities in which you do business. With the rise of big-box retailers, national chains, and e-commerce, endless opportunities now exist to purchase supplies and source products and services.

Because we tend to buy based on price, quality, and convenience, we patronize these giants without much regard to the impact on the local communities in which we do business. But consider that those big companies have a national focus. The more you spend on them, the bigger they grow, while local companies diminish.

Andrew Simms, policy director of the think tank The New Economics Foundation, has measured the impact of national chain stores in the United Kingdom. He says, "The decline in neighborhood shops and service is sounding a death knell across Britain, creating economic ghost towns. . . . Think of your community as a bucket, and think of what's inside that bucket as its wealth. When the consumers and businesses spend outside of that bucket, the wealth leaves, usually forever."

When you buy products online from a national retailer or wholesaler, your money leaks out of the local market. If you hire a national chain to clean your offices, for example, a small percentage stays in town to pay minimum wages while the rest is sent to national headquarters in a different city or even a different state.

Purchasing from locally owned businesses means that the money you spend not only helps the community, but also has a multiplier effect on the good it brings to it. The term "local multiplier effect" was first coined by economist John Maynard Keynes in his 1936 book *The General Theory of Employment, Interest and Money*; it measures how many times dollars recirculate throughout a local economy before leaving it via the purchase of an import. "Imports" means goods or services that come from outside the region, or goods and services purchased from a company headquartered outside the region. The higher the local multiplier effect, the theory goes, the richer and more vibrant the local community becomes.

Recent research confirms this effect: In 2004, the Santa Fe, New Mexico–based research firm Angelou Economics conducted a study that found the impact of dollars spent in an independent business delivered two times the economic impact of spending at national chains. And a 2003 study conducted by Maine's Institute for Local Self-Reliance discovered that 53.3 percent of revenue of locally owned big business stayed in the state, with 44.6 percent of that remaining local and 8.7 percent of it spread statewide. However, less than 15 percent of big-box retailer revenue remained in the state, and what did consisted mainly of low-income wages and minimal taxes.

According to the researchers, this effect occurs for several reasons. On a percentage basis, local businesses contribute more to community charities than their national counterparts. Compared with their giant competitors, local businesses often pay their employees higher wages. They are also more likely to trade with local suppliers or providers. And when local businesses grow, they typically expand locally or in adjacent markets.

Here are a few ways to buy local: Require local alternatives be considered in all of your proposals or purchasing habits. Be willing to pay a small premium. After all, you'll be able to make up for it in quality, consulting with local partners and monitoring the results firsthand.

Join organizations such as the Business Alliance for Local Living Economies (BALLE) or your Local First campaign to tap their resources to source locally. They'll be happy to point you in the right direction and make the networking connections for you.

Use metrics to measure your local multiplier effect on the money your company spends. The New Economics Foundation has a tool called LM3 (available at www.neweconomics.org) that measures three layers of spending. LM3 calculates how many of your purchase dollars leak out of your community, versus those that recirculate.

The more you purchase locally, the more you'll establish vital connections with your community and improve your reputation as a corporate citizen, not just a cohabitant. For example, an October 2000 study by the Produce Marketing Association of approximately one thousand consumers concerning their produce suppliers found that more than half the respondents placed the highest importance on social responsibility and sustainability when choosing a vendor. When researchers measured what constituted responsibility and sustainability, they discovered that distance from the farm to the store was the second most important factor, behind paying a living wage.

When you buy local, you also protect your company from the perils of doing business with distant companies. For example, if oil and gas prices were to spike suddenly, shipping costs would skyrocket, making local purchases cheaper by comparison.

8. Create Local Jobs

Perhaps the best way to connect your company with your community is to generate jobs, as Toyota did in the 1980s by moving some of its production facilities from Japan to the United States. Toyota now enjoys a reputation as a community partner rather than a foreign company.

If it makes sense within the context of your job, make a case for local job creation. Invoke the Law of the Long View and show how, instead of outsourcing to save a penny, your company can earn more in the long run. Research the long-term costs and benefits of staffing and producing products and services locally. Take into account everything from quality control to local taxes, as well as the goodwill you'll create by being a local job creator.

Cessna Aircraft Company, a manufacturer of light aircraft, is headquartered in Wichita, Kansas; its CEO, Russ Meyer, is committed to training locals for every type of job from entry level to executive. Although Cessna is a global operation with 14,000 employees, more than 11,000 of them are located in Wichita, giving the local economy a big boost.

Another community-loyal company is American Apparel, a clothing manufacturer and retailer founded in 1997 by twenty-nine-year-old Dov Charney, a highly controversial business revolutionary. Charney hasn't gotten everything right in his career—he's been heavily criticized for dating female employees and has been the subject of several lawsuits. But his policy of paying above-average wages and providing above-average working conditions has helped his company become wildly successful. More important, he has influenced dozens of other companies in the industry to follow his lead.

Bucking the industry trend to outsource apparel production, Charney built a factory in downtown Los Angeles where the company's entire line is produced. The clothes, product catalogs, and marketing materials are also created on site. Furthermore, the company employs locally, hiring minorities from low-income neighborhoods and paying them more than other garment makers in the city.

In 2006, *Inc.* magazine noted that the company's hiring and compensation policies have generated more-productive employees and a higher-quality product than its competitors'. Because American Apparel manufactures its products locally, managers can inspect products as they come off the line rather than when they arrive en masse from a foreign producer. And local manufacturing allows American Apparel to test and implement design innovations in just a few days. Its competitors, a world away from their production lines, must wait weeks or months to do the same.

The company's locally based humanitarian approach also appeals to ThemGeners. Jane Buckingham, president of the intelligence group that wrote the 2006 *Cassandra Report,* found that American Apparel is one of the top brands among young adults. Brand power translates to sales. Even though American Apparel's products are often priced 20 percent higher than those of its competitors, annual sales have soared—between 2002 and 2005, sales doubled year over year.

9. Locate Business Operations in Impoverished Communities

When a company builds a new factory or service center, it frequently looks for conditions such as a low crime rate, adjacent businesses, modern amenities, and convenience. As a result, most corporate expansion plans follow urban sprawl, locating new operations in affluent or recently developed neighborhoods. Meanwhile, poorer neighborhoods continue to decay.

When Cessna chairman Russ Meyer considered expansion plans in the late 1980s, he knew that the gap between rich and poor in Wichita was widening despite a booming economy. So in 1990, the company launched the 21st Street Program by renovating a vacant grocery store in the 21st Street neighborhood into an aircraft assembly plant. One of the poorest parts of town, the area had high unemployment levels, so the program hired and trained previously low-skilled neighborhood residents for aircraft subassembly positions. Over the next seven years, 90 percent of the participants completed their training programs and became full-time Cessna employees.

Cessna expanded the program in 1997 with a new 21st Street campus complete with subsidized day care, a learning center, and a world-class wellness program.

10. Turn Your Company's Waste into Wealth

Every day at work, you are surrounded by waste that could be easily converted into social nutrition for your community. Have you ever counted all the broken or outdated computers, monitors, printers, phones, desks, and chairs gathering dust?

Many innovators are turning their trash into food by partnering with nonprofit groups with expertise in preparing used items for community distribution.

Electro-Motive, a LaGrange, Illinois—based manufacturer of electric-diesel locomotives, took a novel approach to a recent companywide upgrade of its computers. Instead of throwing out seven hundred old computer workstations, the company donated them to Chicago's Computers for Schools, a nonprofit that refurbishes computers for local school systems. And when executives discovered that the recycling program was popular with employees, they organized a three-day recycling drive. Employee enthusiasm was so high that organizers created a follow-up event for the general public at Chicago's United Center. Between the two events, more than 80,000 pounds of computer and office equipment were collected.

Don't stop at computers. In Lynchburg, Virginia, the local nonprofit Crayons to Computers works with dozens of local businesses to redistribute unused or discarded office supplies, equipment, and furniture to community area schools. Similarly, Maryland farmer Rod Parker lets the Washington Area Gleaning Network, a local nonprofit that feeds the needy, pick over his farm after the annual harvest. As a farmer, he's committed to feeding people, and he derives satisfaction from knowing his unpicked items are being put to good use. Larry's Markets in Seattle donates expired or dented canned goods to local food banks. Fletcher Allen Healthcare, a medical center in Vermont, donates unused produce from its cafeteria to local nonprofits that feed the homeless.

Your company meetings and events may provide you with an opportunity to give back to your local community as well. I've attended hundreds of them over the last few years as a public speaker, and I'm always amazed how much food is wasted. In the fall of 2007, the socially minded rock band Phish, along with event vendors, donated all the edible leftover food from its concert in Limestone, Maine, to Catholic Charities Maine. The results were not trivial: Volunteers collected more than $5,000 worth of frozen, dry, and canned food.

11. Increase Your Personal Community Value

In the new global economy, it's easy to become focused on national news and international networking. As you've read through these advice points, perhaps you've come up empty when it comes to local opportunities. What can you do?

Go on a learning spree by following local news, subscribing to the local newspaper, and attending town meetings or chamber of commerce functions. Do some Internet research to learn more about your community's history. Network with area business owners and professionals, and attend community functions. Make it a goal to add at least one community member to your personal contacts every month.

By deepening your involvement with your community, you'll become aware of social opportunities with which your company can connect. Along the way, you'll also improve your assessment of your company's social performance in the local community, a good starting point for making a difference locally.

12

Act: Save Your Planet

Peter and Laurie Danis of Columbus, Ohio, have owned their family restaurant, Figlio, since 1992. Recently, their sixteen-year-old daughter, Cameron, started working at the restaurant, busing tables and doing odd jobs.

After noticing that the restaurant's trash barrels were filled with wine bottles, recyclable plastic, and cardboard containers, Cameron confronted her father at the dinner table, saying, "I can't believe we're not recycling. Dad, do you realize that all this is just going to get buried in a landfill? This is very bad for the environment!"

"Figlio is a small business," her father replied. "What can I do in the bigger scheme of things?"

"For sixteen years," Cameron said, "you've been telling me that we all have a gift, and that we all have to find a way to use our gift to make a difference in the world. You made Figlio the first nonsmoking restaurant in Columbus. You influenced other restaurants, it became a local movement, and now it's the law. You were just one restaurant then. Look what you were able to do!"

His daughter's words lit a fire beneath Danis, who quickly located a Toronto-based company that helped him institute a recycling program. He found that he could purchase renewable-energy credits to offset the carbon emissions created by his restaurants (he now has three); these credits would help fund regional development of wind and solar power. Even though it cost several thousands of dollars, he wrote a check for a year's work of offsets.

Next he went after his electricity consumption by installing energy-efficient, compact fluorescent lightbulbs and by initiating staff meetings to discuss ideas to conserve energy.

During the 2006 holiday season, Danis sent out his last batch of paper greeting cards to his customers, along with a note telling them that in the future, his cards would be digital.

A few months into Danis's eco-transformation, he attended a local restaurant association meeting, where he shared some of his new green business practices. Other restaurant owners chimed in with helpful ideas, including energy-saving tips, places to buy local produce, and ways to reduce transportation emissions.

Danis adopted several of these ideas and continued to bring the issue to the forefront at future meetings—all of which earned him a cover story in *Biz First*, a local business news publication, and in turn led to a late-2007 story in *USA Today*. And all because his daughter believed that being green at work was "the only right thing to do."

Whether you work for a small business or a massive enterprise, you can improve your company's environmental effectiveness. As mentioned, Interface's Ray Anderson calls this journey "climbing Mount Sustainability"; he maintains that it will not be accomplished by a single breakthrough or even a couple of companywide innovations. Creating a sustainable company requires hundreds of small, personal innovations, with everyone contributing to a companywide culture. That reality makes each and every employee vital, and your daily practices significant.

The advice below is divided into two sections: ways to reduce your personal footprint and ways to reduce your company's footprint. Both will help your company, which in turn will save it money and improve its reputation.

Personal Footprint

Much of your company's greenhouse-gas-emission footprint results from the personal behavior of its employees. According to Michael Totten, senior director of climate at the Center for Environmental Leadership in Business, "Three numbers will dominate most organizations' footprint: energy used in the building, employee travel, and paper consumption."

Of the three mentioned, paper consumption represents one of the easiest to address. Although the Information Age promised us a paperless office, the reality is that we print more pages every day than ever before.

In their booklet *Paper Cuts: Recovering the Paper Landscape*, environmental researchers Janet Abramovitz and Ashley Mattoon document that the number of pages printed in American offices increases by 20 percent annually, due to the explosion of information and printer accessibility. As of 2008, the average worker in America prints one piece of paper every ten minutes.

Each stage of the printing-paper supply chain attacks the environment. Harvesting timber for paper pulp threatens forests and species. Processing pulp to paper generates wastewater and consumes massive amounts of petroleum. Transporting paper, a heavy item in bulk, consumes gasoline and contributes to air pollution. Even the ink used for printing carries its own environmental price tag, as it requires oil and produces gases and toxins if not properly disposed.

Consider some alarming facts from a 2006 report by the Environmental Paper Network, a research consortium of leading corporations and nonprofit groups related to the paper industry. Forests store over half of the world's terrestrial carbon. Environmental experts call forests the sponge that absorbs carbon emissions and keeps the world in balance. More than 40 percent of industrial wood harvesting supports the paper industry, of which more than 60 percent is used for document printing.

The paper industry is the primary consumer of water in developed countries. Paper accounts for one-fourth of the volume of waste in landfills. When it breaks down in a landfill, it converts to methane, which produces twenty times more greenhouse-gas emissions than carbon dioxide. If the United States cut annual paper use by 20 percent, it would prevent the emission of more than 3 million tons of greenhouse gases—the equivalent of taking half a million cars off the road for a year.

So roll up your sleeves and redesign how you consume and distribute information. Personally, I've reduced my paper footprint by more than 50 percent over the last year, despite the fact that I've been researching and writing a book. The following five pieces of advice can help you do the same—or better.

1. Use Recycled Paper

Partially or fully recycled paper has far less impact than virgin-timber paper. A 2002 study by the Alliance for Environmental Innovation determined that using recycled paper stock will enable you to eliminate wood use and reduce net greenhouse-gas emissions by 50 percent and wastewater by 33 percent.

Some of you may not like the quality of 100 percent recycled paper. If so, bridge that gap with 30 percent recycled paper stock, which retains the brightness and thickness of virgin paper but still puts a dent in your paper footprint. The research mentioned above determined that for every forty cases of 30 percent recycled paper stock you substitute for virgin stock, you save more than seven trees and preserve more than 2,000 gallons of water from being used in the production process.

Find out what kind of paper your printers or copiers use. Talk to your office manager and share these numbers on environmental impact. Often, as is the case with office supercenters Staples and OfficeMax, the price difference between virgin and recycled paper is less than 10 percent, and it's dropping steadily.

2. Think Before You Print

Over the course of the last few decades, we've gotten into a habit: We print, then think. Instead, we should think first and only then print—maybe.

Let's say you receive a PDF document, print it, and then realize it's a fifty-page tome that you really didn't want to read. Or you get a bloated PowerPoint presentation or a ten-page e-mail. What do you do? Print to read it later, and then discover it's one hundred pages long, or nothing you needed to see, or perhaps that it wasn't even meant for you in the first place.

Try a new professional practice: Make every print job beg for its life. Put up a sign on your printer that reads, "Think Before You Print."

When you do decide to print, scrutinize the page count. How many pages is the document—and how many does it have to be? For example, when printing an e-mail conversation, you may find it runs twenty pages, when all you need is the last few exchanges. The same goes for an online map: Frequently, you'll find it prints on a single page but is followed by a second, third, or even fourth, all littered with advertisements. Reformat documents to eliminate wasted pages, or read them on-screen and skip the print job altogether.

With PowerPoint presentations, typically one page per slide, a fifty-slide presentation prints at fifty pages. There's an alternative: Click Print on the file menu, find the drop-down menu titled Print What? Click it and select Handouts instead of Slides (the default setting). That way, you can print up to twelve handouts per page, depending on their size.

Help coworkers break their bad habits with a Think Before You Print sign as well. A sales coordinator at a Pasadena mortgage company took this idea a step further. To see how effective these signs could be, not just on his own behavior but on that of his entire floor, he conducted an experiment in which he counted how many reams of paper his floor used in one week. The following week he posted Think Before You Print signs in bold letters on all the floor's common printers. Underneath, he included his e-mail address for any questions. The next week, he counted the reams used—printing was down 20 percent. Then he posted a larger sign, and the total reduction zoomed to almost 40 percent.

3. Print on Both Sides of the Page

Another simple way to reduce your paper footprint is to set printing to duplex mode, or printing on both sides of the page. In 2006, office workers for the City of Seattle reduced their paper printing by more than 21 percent using duplex-mode copying and printing.

If duplex-mode printing isn't possible because you use a small printer, you can cut your paper use manually by using two-sided printing. Take used, unneeded paper, turn it over, and print on the other side. For many, your printing is primarily for your eyes only, and reusing such paper will reduce the amount of fresh paper you need.

I shared this idea with owners of a small marketing agency in Burbank, California. Not long after they started printing two-sided by reusing paper before recycling it, they actually ran out of waste-paper. So they canvassed all twelve tenants in their office building and collected hundreds of pages of discarded paper that had already been printed on one side. This new system has helped the agency reduce the amount of paper it purchases by more than 50 percent.

4. Recycle

When paper has run its course, has been printed on both sides, and is no longer useful, it should be properly recycled. This is the only responsible way to dispose of wastepaper. Otherwise, it ends up in a garbage dump where it will decompose, releasing methane, a greenhouse gas twenty times more damaging to the environment than carbon dioxide. This means that whenever we put paper in the trash, we're contributing to global warming.

You should recycle not only documents but old phone books, product manuals, and the endless loads of catalogs and junk mail that stream into your office. Absent your attention, many of them will likely end up in a Dumpster and make their way into your local landfill.

Be careful how you recycle waste. The process becomes inefficient when waste-management workers must separate different materials such as paper, aluminum, and plastic from trash bins because each one requires a different process to recycle. To minimize the energy required for recycling, be conscientious about what goes where. If you don't have a dedicated bin for paper, ask for one.

Now that you're recycling, remember that it's a disposal method, not a license to use all the paper you want. According to McDonough and Braungart in *Cradle to Cradle,* recycling should really be called downcycling, because the quality and usefulness of paper decrease every time it is recycled. This means that even with recycling, our paper use drives the demand for timber harvesting and pulp processing, both of which are harmful to the environment.

5. Reduce Others' Paper Footprint

However you personally use paper, your footprint may be much larger than you think because you are requiring others to overprint.

You may have learned to think before you print, but many others haven't. They'll open anything you send them, and often print it out without considering page count.

Redesign documents to print on fewer pages. Preview documents before sending them to calculate the page count. If you find pages with only a sentence or two on them, change the font or format to squeeze a one-and-a-half-page document onto a single page. When sending out a PowerPoint presentation, consider formatting it as a handout with multiple slides per page.

If you use Adobe Acrobat PDF documents (the fastest-growing category in business), encourage people to read them on-screen. Visit GreenPDF.com, a Web site at which you can download a free tool that inserts a little pop-up box into your PDF telling the reader not to print it.

Similarly, ask that presentations be delivered electronically rather than on paper. Often, people automatically run to the local Kinko's or hit their copier and print out a two-hundred-page report that could just as easily be read on-screen.

Another indirect way you may be increasing your paper footprint is through inaction. Typically, an endless stream of paper runs through your office: junk mail, catalogs, sales presentations, and magazines. Visit Web sites such as EcologicalMail.org and take yourself and your coworkers off junk-mail and catalog lists. Don't forget to do this every time someone leaves your company. For each person you successfully remove from mailing lists, you will conserve trees, save your company handling fees, and prevent pounds of solid waste.

All of these techniques will help redesign your business life to generate less printing—and your example may inspire others to do the same.

The next five points speak to your non-paper-related personal work footprint and will help you and your company become more environmentally, financially, and socially efficient. Companies that use less electricity and fewer petroleum-based products will have a better carbon-footprint rating on future product labels.

In the future, when carbon taxes are passed—as they are likely to be—eco-minded companies will suffer less than their not-so-green competitors. That's why your efforts to protect the environment by reducing your footprint are not only socially responsible, they are good business practices in line with the Law of the Ledger.

6. *Become an Energy Saver*

When you were young, your parents probably told you to turn off the lights. But now that you're an adult, do you turn off the lights at work when you leave for the day?

According to a 2007 national survey conducted by Harris Interactive for Sun Microsystems, 92 percent of respondents said they turn off the lights when they leave a room at home, but only 52 percent said they do so at work. Dave Douglas, vice president of eco-responsibility at Sun Microsystems, says, "Businesses don't cut power consumption. People do. If you're an employee . . . you have an enormous opportunity to make a difference for our planet."

So turn off all the lights when you leave for the day. And don't stop with the lights. Turn off computers, copiers, and printers in your cubicle and, if appropriate, your office. Each one of those devices, when left on standby or plugged into a power strip, drains up to seventy watts of continuous electricity. Recent research conducted by the EPA shows that you can cut your electrical consumption by 10 percent by powering off devices and turning off power strips.

Some people believe turning everything off at night, and then back on the following day, wears out on-and-off switches. But according to Pat Turner, a facilities manager at the University of Maryland, "If you have equipment for more than ten years, this may be the case. But in reality . . . you change almost all of your equipment every few years, long before any on/off switches can wear out with overuse."

Likewise, monitor and adjust your habits concerning heat and air-conditioning. The energy used to heat or cool buildings is a big driver of a company's carbon footprint. Resist the temptation to crank up the AC or heater at work. Bring a sweater during the winter; dress light during the summer. On a hot summer day, draw the blinds shut in the morning to keep the heat out. On a cold but sunny winter day, open them and let the sun heat the room.

7. Reduce Transportation Emissions
As mentioned, research by the Center for Environmental Leadership in Business has determined that employee travel constitutes a major part of a company's carbon footprint.

So slash it. The next time you're taking a meeting out of the office, ask yourself—do you really need to go? Yes, you can easily jump in a car or grab a cheap regional flight and get some face time. But have you exhausted the alternatives? An inexpensive videoconference can mimic the benefits of a personal meeting, as can, in some instances, a simple conference call.

When you absolutely have to travel, try to reduce long-haul air travel. In 2005, researchers at the environmental consultant AEA Technology found that one long-haul airplane trip will create significantly more carbon emissions than your car does in an entire year.

In your daily commute, use mass transit whenever possible. Many companies offer vouchers to support mass transit. Investigate carpooling as well.

Many of your other business habits create transportation-related carbon emissions. For example, some workers suffer from Overnight Shipping Syndrome, using next-day air delivery for every package. Air freight is the most carbon-intensive form of shipping; air shipping's footprint is much bigger than that of ground or marine shipping.

Aveda Corporation's own internal study revealed that shipping by air emitted seventy-three times more carbon dioxide than shipping by sea, so the company now uses sea rather than air freight whenever possible.

8. Reduce Waste

Simple daily acts such as having a drink of water or grabbing a quick lunch can create a tremendous amount of waste. For example, the production of the bottles in bottled water, along with long-haul transportation to get them to your door, creates significant carbon emissions.

Research by the Pacific Institute reveals that, in 2006, "producing the [water] bottles for American consumption required the equivalent of more than seventeen million barrels of oil [annually], not including the energy for transportation." It takes three liters of fresh water to produce one liter of bottled water.

Instead of using bottled water, bring a refillable water container and refill it at a water fountain or sink. If your company has a water cooler, ask your facilities group to install a water filter instead. This way, you'll reduce the energy required to pick up, refill, transport, and manufacture the large containers.

Similarly, when eating, don't use disposable utensils. If you can't find metalware, consider keeping your own utensils on hand and set an example for others.

When it comes to larger equipment, repair rather than replace. Our habit of throwing away, and then replacing, electronic devices puts a strain on landfills and triggers more production, which in turn requires energy and raw materials. According to author Paul Hawken, as of 1999, 40,000 pounds of waste was created to produce a single ten-pound laptop.

Resist the temptation to upgrade to the latest and greatest piece of office equipment just for newness's sake. Do you really need it if you've been using the one you have without a problem? Leading social innovators, from SAS Institute to Google, have learned that by delaying equipment upgrades, they avoid wasting hundreds or thousands of useful devices without hindering business performance.

When you must dispose of unfixable items, be responsible. Most computer manufacturers will take them back at little or no expense; the same goes for cell phones. Visit the manufacturer's Web site to look for disposal options. If your company offers recycling only for paper and plastic items, talk to your facilities or waste-management team about disposal options for electronics and office equipment such as furniture.

9. Buy Offsets Whenever Possible

Some companies allow employees to buy renewable-energy credits that offset their business air travel or total work-related carbon footprint. These credits are given by accredited nonprofits in exchange for contributions made to the development of alternative energy. Credits are customarily calculated based on the carbon emissions generated by a specific trip or activity.

If your company offers this option, take advantage; if it doesn't, seek permission to start a program.

Buying offsets allows you to form the habit of paying for carbon emissions. Environmental consultant Amory Lovins believes that the reason we use so much energy is that it's too cheap. By purchasing offsets, you raise the ante and also condition yourself to expect to be charged whenever you don't save energy.

Finally, when you buy offsets, your investment helps to develop renewable-energy sources, whether it's solar, wind, or other alternatives to petroleum—all of which may help turn the tide and eliminate our dependence on petroleum, coal, and other forms of polluting energy.

Carbon-offset solutions are easy to locate. For example, carbonfund.org allows you to calculate and purchase offsets on an individual basis, as do thegreenoffice.com and climatecare.org.

10. Choose Virtual Over Physical

Do you use an electronic voice-mail system or a personal answering machine? The latter is the Hummer of communications technology. Hundreds of pounds of carbon emissions go into its production process, and when thrown out, it can emit hazardous substances. The voice mail offered by almost every phone-services provider is a much greener option.

Instead of buying an extra hard drive to back up data on your computer, use one of many online solutions that offer inexpensive backup, such as LiveVault.com or DataDepositBox.com. Similarly, when purchasing software, use the online download-install option instead of having compact discs sent to you. Download the PDF of the user's manual and save it to your hard drive.

Whenever possible, conduct virtual meetings with your business partners. Hold a video or telephone conference, conduct a LiveMeeting, or exchange electronic documents. Unless it's unavoidable, don't ask people—including vendors—to travel to you. You'll save them time and, in most cases, produce the same business results.

Not only will you make a difference by reducing emissions of carbon and other pollutants, you'll be influencing others to think in new ways.

Company Footprint

Now that you've worked on your personal footprint, it's time to help your company climb Mount Sustainability.

The phrase "sustainable development," first coined by the 1987 World Commission on Environment and Development, is defined as "development that meets the needs of the present without compromising the ability of future generations to meet their own needs."

In applying this concept to the business world, I define sustainability as a company's ability to engage in business practices responsibly and indefinitely. This credo applies across its products, services, and operations.

Being green—that is, sustainable—will be vital to your company during the Responsibility Revolution. A November 2007 survey of college students and entry-level workers conducted by employment Web site Monster.com revealed that more than nine of ten employees are "more inclined to work for a company that is environmentally friendly."

At the other end of the age spectrum, green is also seen as important in terms of brand loyalty. A December 2007 survey conducted by research firm Focalyst for the American Association of Retired

People found that more than 40 million Americans can be classified as "green boomers," consumers who purchase products that are greener or are made by companies with a track record of being green in their operations.

Whatever your job—facilities manager, building engineer, human resources manager, product designer, transportation manager, purchasing agent, office manager, and so on—you can have significant influence on your company's sustainability.

11. Hire Eco-Friendly People

Ed Catmull, president of Pixar and Disney Animation Studios, once asked me: "What's more important to a successful project, great ideas or great people?" His own answer: people. After all, if you take a perfect idea but give it to four incompetent people, it will fail.

If you want your company to go green, first search for green-friendly employees, as Timberland does when selecting business managers; its recruiting manager, Liam Connelly, says that when interviewing MBA graduates, he looks beyond their finance or marketing skills for people who "have a passion to make the world a better place."

During job interviews at companies such as Green Mountain Coffee Roasters and Patagonia, candidates are queried about their environmental interests and passions during job interviews. Similarly, a 2007 *Wall Street Journal*/Harris Interactive survey found that eight out of ten corporate recruiters search out business managers who have knowledge of, and interest in, sustainability.

Include sustainability in your hiring process, too. When advertising jobs, mention that you're looking for eco-friendly applicants. Add sections on your employment form in which candidates must write an essay about their concern for the environment or list eco-friendly activities in which they participate. Emphasize green values in the hiring criteria, along with education, experience, and attitude. When you hire people because of their passion for the environment, make sure to tell them to bring these sensibilities to work.

Hiring eco-minded employees will not only ensure they'll practice sustainability but will also help you live by the Law of the Ledger. Such workers will use less electricity, produce less waste, and reduce your future liabilities by instinctively acting to preserve the environment in all they do.

12. Promote Eco-Friendly Employee Habits
One of the first components in Wal-Mart's companywide sustainability initiative was employee education. To implement this mandate, the company hired Adam Werbach, former president of the Sierra Club and current CEO of Act Now, a sustainability training company.

Each year, Werbach trains thousands of Wal-Mart managers and employees on the fundamentals of sustainability, helping them to create their own PSPs (personal sustainability projects), a process that heightens their sensitivity to the environment. The PSPs reinforce the company initiative, increase employee engagement, and spur innovative thinking at the store level.

Make eco-studies part of your new-hire orientation process. Bring in an expert to conduct a workshop. Offer to reimburse employees who take environmental studies classes at a local college or through a training company.

You can also promote green thinking at work through compensation programs. Timberland and Google award employees up to $5,000 for buying a hybrid car. Wal-Mart includes energy-efficiency and sustainability metrics in managers' annual evaluations and bonus plans.

Find creative ways to reward green behavior at work. For example, create an eco-profit-sharing plan, where you calculate money saved by employee contributions to sustainability, then share the windfall with them, like a profit-sharing plan. The more you reward, the more you motivate.

13. Green Up Your Buildings
Next to hiring the right people, making buildings more energy efficient is the most important step in a company's journey up Mount Sustainability. The EPA estimates that buildings consume two-thirds of all electricity in the United States; they also create more than one-third of carbon dioxide emissions, a higher percentage than that of automobiles.

A common notion in the construction and design industry is that green buildings start with energy efficiency. Stuart Brodsky, national program manager for Energy Star, a joint program of the Department of Energy and the EPA, points out that "the energy consumed by a building over its life exponentially exceeds the energy and fossil fuels consumed for the building's materials and development."

To green up your building, start out by doing a building checkup of your company at the Web site EnergyStar.gov. Its Portfolio Manager lets you compare the energy efficiency of your building to similar ones across the nation and identify areas where you can improve. Brodsky also suggests you inspect your facility to make sure light, heat, and air are evenly distributed.

As mentioned previously, you can increase energy efficiency, as well as lift moods, by bringing sunshine into the workplace, through installing sloped ceilings, atriums, skylights, and light reflectors on the roofs. Lockheed Missile and Space Company's facility in Sunnyvale, California, installed such daylighting solutions throughout its buildings and cut its electricity use by 75 percent in one year.

Make sure you employ light dimmers and sensors, programmed

to adjust lighting automatically. Texas Instruments, for one, installed new dimmers and sensors in its north Texas facilities and decreased its energy use by 80 percent.

Next, look for the Energy Star rating on equipment and appliances you purchase or lease. These ratings guarantee the maximum level of energy efficiency available and in many cases also qualify you for tax credits or deductions. Finally, consider your building's water efficiency. State agriculture departments from California to Connecticut predict dire water shortages over the next decade, so it's vital to act now. Install auto-off faucets in bathrooms and recycle wastewater through landscape sprinkler systems. Think about rocks or sculptures instead of grass for lawns; install drainage solutions to use rainwater whenever possible.

For new building projects, seek out sustainable building materials. In this case, sustainable means inexhaustible, or products that are renewable or recycled as opposed to made from, say, petroleum products or virgin timber. Ask your suppliers to give you an accounting of all materials used in your building supplies and specify to what level they are sustainable. When you write up requests for proposals (RFPs) for contractors, stipulate that you prefer such materials.

To minimize waste, emulate nature by allowing for artistic imperfections in pattern-matching in woods, textiles, and surfaces. Much carpet waste occurs during installation, when patterns don't line up correctly and good carpet is discarded. Interface introduced a random-pattern carpet to solve this problem, and the company has reduced installation-related waste by more than 90 percent in office buildings where it was selected over standard carpet.

Similarly, choose natural woods versus clear-grain, or perfect, woods. In his book *Deep Economy*, Bill McKibben notes that when Middlebury College used natural woods, students and faculty often stopped to admire it for its character and charm, proving that one building designer's trash is another's treasure.

14. Screen New Products for Environmental Impact

Most of us can analyze new products and services for profitability and quality. But how rigorously can you screen a product for its environmental impact?

Merely examining whether the product or service complies with current environmental regulations isn't enough. Decades ago, General Electric carefully followed the letter of the law in its power-plant-manufacturing operations and ended up polluting the Hudson River and creating hundreds of millions of dollars of liability.

Harking back to the Law of the Long View, improve your eco-product screening process through scenario planning. Imagine a future world where carbon emission taxes have been instituted. Envision a law that has created a market for carbon emissions, whereby companies with high levels have to buy credits from companies in their own industry that have outperformed them in this area. How will the product you're now considering contribute to your company's carbon footprint? How would it stack up against a competitor's?

Here's how Interface does a scenario planning: When presented with a product or service plan, the company's product developers look at each step of the product life cycle and ask, "What happens next?"

If you ask this question enough, you may well discover you don't know the eco-risks; worse, you may discover that your product has the potential to do the most damage when it reaches the end of its useful life in the distant future. In these cases, you might want to rethink your strategy.

At Aveda, they call this assessment the "mission-aligned product-review process." As Horst Rechelbacher told his product-development employees, "If you have any questions between what I say and what the environmental research says, report to the planet."

15. Increase Your Products' Sustainability

In my view, anything that you sell to a customer is a product, whether it's a physical object or a service. And sustainability, a powerful reflection of a company's responsibility, is about to become the new basis for competition among products. Your product's sustainability will determine your company's brand strength as well as its long-term level of financial stability.

Sustainable products don't rely on ingredients that are in short supply, such as dwindling natural resources.

Renewable energy and recycled or recyclable materials are examples of highly sustainable ingredients, because they can either be reused or regenerated.

The quest for such sustainable products starts with a hard look at their ingredients. Every product has two kinds: human ingredients, from ideas to labor; and technical ingredients, or the physical materials that constitute the product.

In "Save Your People," I talked about sustainable practices regarding human labor. Now let's look at being environmentally sustainable in terms of technical ingredients.

If you operate a janitorial service, for example, your technical ingredients are your workers' cleaning supplies. If you run a chair-making operation, your technical ingredients may be woods, plastics, fabrics, and metals.

To be sustainable, these ingredients must be renewable or in ample supply. Or they must be infinitely recyclable, reused, or reclaimed. Paper, as discussed, is a nonrenewable ingredient; because its quality breaks down every time it is recycled, only a small percentage of paper is recovered for reuse.

On the other hand, aluminum is a very sustainable ingredient. It is upcyclable, meaning that it can be recycled indefinitely with no loss of quality, and the process requires little energy. Furthermore, many aluminum recyclers now use wind and solar power for their conversion process.

You can't determine how sustainable ingredients are, however, if you can't trace where they come from or how they were processed or manufactured. Aveda had to learn that lesson; as mentioned earlier, the sandalwood oil in their Love-Perfume product was poached from forests in East India.

To analyze your product's sustainability, use a free tool designed for manufacturers of physical products, built and offered by the West Michigan Business Forum. It's downloadable at www.wmsbf.org/downloads/desguide.pdf.

If along the way you find ingredients that are unsustainable, seek ways to create your product using renewable ingredients. Daniel Esty and Andrew Winston, authors of Green to Gold, interviewed executives and product developers at IKEA, the home and office furniture maker, and found that its innovation had moved from aesthetic design to product sustainability. Product designers now think: How can we make furniture when there is no oil and gas?

The next ingredient to consider on your product's path to sustainability is the one added by your customer. For example, for their product to work, automakers require customers to add gasoline, and gasoline constitutes the largest part of an automaker's carbon footprint.

Electronics manufacturers are increasingly designing computers, wireless phones, and entertainment devices that go into power hibernation when not in use. And in the near future, we'll be seeing product designs that use renewable energy, such as solar-powered wireless phones. We'll also see products designed much like the old-fashioned mechanical watch, where the customer-added ingredient is physical effort rather than a battery.

Next, consider the packaging of your product; by sheer volume, packaging is often one of its main ingredients. Some products contain more packaging than actual product. Most of it exists to increase the product's perceived value, or to protect it from theft, tampering, or breakage.

Besides being wasteful, a great deal of hard-plastic safety packaging is made from unsustainable ingredients such as polyvinyl chloride (PVC). PVC also contains numerous toxins that are shed when it is discarded or ends up in a landfill. In addition, most of this plastic is treated as trash and thrown away, rather than sent off for recycling.

Companies can increase their products' sustainability through redesign, as computer company Hewlett-Packard did in 2006 with its bestselling printer-ink cartridges. HP made its product packaging smaller and lighter, which reduced the total carbon footprint of each cartridge. The redesign also replaced PVC with recyclable non-toxic plastic resins, preventing 6.8 million pounds of PVC from going into landfills annually. The redesign of this single line of products reduced HP's greenhouse-gas emissions by an estimated 37 million pounds in 2007—the equivalent of taking 3,600 cars off the road for one year. HP also includes small envelopes with its cartridges so users can send them back for recycling.

You can also effect radical redesign in packaging by making the package reusable. One of the greatest consumer innovations of the last few years is the reusable cloth grocery bag, which replaces throw-away packaging (paper and plastic bags). Taking a cue, Microsoft redesigned the hard-plastic clamshells that protect its electronics and software, which are used for security reasons, especially for small but valuable electronic devices.

For its 2007 Streets & Trips GPS device, Microsoft used recycled as well as recyclable plastics to produce its security clamshell. The company then went one step further, making the plastic clamshell reusable as a protective tool to hold the GPS when it wasn't mounted to the customer's car dashboard. This redesign reduced the negative environmental impacts for this product by more than 75 percent and dramatically improved its sustainability.

16. Green Up Your Partners

Your suppliers, distributors, and resellers play an important role in your products' sustainability. If their practices, from repackaging to transporting your products, are unsustainable, they factor into your company's total eco-footprint.

Assess your supply chain from an environmental standpoint. Your chain comprises all the organizations, materials, and efforts that move your product from its source to the customer. As mentioned earlier, after an evaluation of their print-production practices, executives at *Time* magazine discovered that a single paper mill was creating 30 percent of the company's footprint.

You must be mindful of your supply chain's contribution to carbon-emissions levels, because regulators, SRI fund managers, and watchdog groups will analyze its environmental impact going forward even if you don't.

To help you do this, global consulting firm Supply Chain Consulting offers a free analytical tool at www.carbon-view.com that helps you determine your carbon footprint, taking into account all your supply-chain partners.

Make sure to communicate environmental goals with your partners and share your assessment of their impact on your product's sustainability. Host a summit to share your eco-vision (and think about using interactive video technology rather than flying everyone in).

Another way to green up your supply chain is to base part of your choice of partners on their level of eco-effectiveness. For example, hospitality chain Wyndham Hotels makes sustainability the tiebreaker when it chooses soaps and shampoos for its hotel rooms; the company's purchasing agents also select green cleaning products for their janitorial staff.

17. Cut Transportation Emissions

Transportation emissions represent another significant segment of your company's footprint. These emissions include everything from employee travel to the transportation of materials along the supply chain.

One way to reduce them is to let employees telecommute whenever feasible, which can be very attractive to prospective employees who don't want to drive long distances.

If you have a corporate campus, offer mass transit by subsidizing monthly rider fees; if the bus stop or transit station is more than a few blocks from your company, provide shuttle services to your front door.

Purchase hybrid company cars and/or give employees a bonus for purchasing one for personal use. If you own fleets, look into purchasing or leasing clean diesel or hybrid diesel trucks.

Another way to cut transportation emissions is to shorten the distance your materials or products must travel through the supply chain. When Wal-Mart considers how far food is transported, it calculates food miles and tries to reduce them over time, considering them an environmental expense.

Look for suppliers located close to your company or its customers. The more you reduce product miles, the more you reduce your carbon footprint. However, when choosing local alternatives, take into account their production process to make sure you're maintaining the same level of total eco-efficiency as you currently receive from regional or international suppliers. Sometimes a small local provider may have a production inefficiency that dilutes the environmental advantages of its proximity.

18. Discard Responsibly

Every product's life cycle ends with the question of disposal. Think about product disposal as an important stakeholder service, like customer service.

Offer to take back products at the end of their useful life, and manage recycling and disposal as a natural part of your business operations, similar to marketing and finance. As Dell learned, failure to do so could hurt your company's social reputation.

One quick way to address the disposal issue is to design products to be environmentally neutral when they are thrown out, eliminating the concept of waste in your product's life cycle. Environmental attorney Joan Krajewski, the unofficial eco-leader at Microsoft, says, "When it comes to packaging, we're looking at different materials, we're doing tests on reusing potato skins, we're looking at different biodegradable materials such as corn starch and sugar."

If the company is successful in this initiative, then it no longer has to rely on customers to recycle. Author William McDonough has developed a biodegradable bottle that has a seed in its lining, so when it's discarded, it potentially plants a tree.

19. Give Your Customers an Eco Option

In 1989, Boston's Lennox Hotel, part of the Saunders Hotel Group, introduced the first towel and linen reuse program when the general manager had placards placed in every guest bathroom that read: "By hanging your towels back up instead of leaving them on the floor, you can use them again, and we'll save water, we'll reduce pollution, and we'll help save the planet."

Customers enthusiastically participated, and the program spread throughout the Saunders Group hotels. Within a few years, the American Hotel and Lodging Association accelerated its growth by creating the Good Earthkeeping program, subsequently adopted by tens of thousands of hotels worldwide.

On behalf of the association, Project Planet Corporation now distributes hundreds of thousands of these placards annually to hotels around the world. The company also conducts research to measure the social and financial impacts of towel and linen reuse programs. According to Patricia Skozelas, vice president of Project Planet, "Between 68 and 72 percent of guests elect to participate. Environmentally, [the program] saves 6,000 gallons of water and 40 gallons of detergent monthly in one 150-room hotel."

By the late 1990s banks, too, were riding the eco-customer wave, as many started offering no-receipt ATM transactions, preventing thousands of pounds of paper from being printed out and discarded every year. Every national bank now offers customers the option of paperless monthly statements as well.

Retail stores, too, got the message: Grocery store chains such as Ralph's and Trader Joe's sell reusable cloth grocery bags; Ralph's customers receive a small rebate every time they use one. Even apparel retailers such as Barney's are giving customers a reusable bag with an eco-friendly message on it.

Whatever program you implement, consider offering customers a choice to do good, rather than making it mandatory. If you cut out paper statements or fresh towels without asking, some customers might perceive the change as a drop in their level of service. Instead, let them participate in the decision.

20. Adopt a Rival's Innovation
Live by the Law of Abundance. Review your assessment from the beginning of this section. Did you read about one of your competitors' green innovations? Did you feel like calling them, finding out how they did it, and bringing it to your workplace? Or were you filled with scarcity thinking, deciding that you weren't interested because the idea didn't originate at your company?

If you reach out to your competitors for help, you might be surprised to find out that they are happy to share their innovations. Again, as the sign on the front door of Patagonia's headquarters declares, "There is no business to be done on a dead planet."

Now that you're ready to green up your business, it's time to get a handle on your carbon-footprint fitness. Several online resources are available to help you. Climatecare.org/calculators/business offers a tool that calculates your carbon footprint based on your company office and employee travel practices. Thegreenoffice.com/carbon offers a calculator that gauges an entire office's emissions. After instituting green practices, try the calculators again, and rejoice in the improvement!

13

Influence

I hope you've spotted several appropriate social opportunities for your company in this book. But you may be hesitating because you don't have control over your budget, the authority to approve a sponsorship, or the power to change the culture of your company. You're wondering what you can do.

Few of us have the power to change policy absolutely, but all of us have the power to effect change through the power of influence. That which you cannot do directly yourself can be accomplished with the creation of a team. Saver soldiers realize that it's imperative to persuade others to join in making a difference as they make a dollar. Influence multiplies the value of knowledge.

You might have already found ways to cut your personal footprint at work. What if you convinced others to join in? What kind of impact would that have? Or perhaps you can invent new ways to support your employees and coworkers. Would others at your company participate? How would that transform your company's reputation as an employer?

When you take on the challenge of influencing others, you are stepping up as a leader during a time of change.

Here are some tips on how to help lead others, starting with the most basic form of influence: evangelizing, or spreading the good word.

1. Evangelize

In the context of business, evangelism signifies your personal campaign to bring about change. It arises from your deep passion to make a difference, combined with a strategic understanding of the area in which you want to see that change.

Whether you're pitching a facilities manager on green buildings or a marketing director on community services, you must know how to transform minds and behavior. I've had a chance to talk with dozens of saver soldiers who were credited with evangelizing a social innovation at work, and helping others to adopt it. Along the way, I've identified three basic rules for effective evangelism.

Teach, Don't Preach

In the business world, you must use finesse when challenging the status quo; this point is especially crucial if you're ahead of the revolutionary curve.

The task of saving people, communities, or the planet is emotionally charged. It's easy to feel that you know best, and you want to beat people over the head with your knowledge—and in so doing, you may find you inadvertently make others feel bad about themselves. This is not the way to move people to action. Careful instruction is.

First, be well informed so you have the depth of knowledge required to answer tough questions.

Communicate clearly. Talk in specific but easy-to-understand terms. Use relevant examples. Stay away from jargon, slogans, or bromides. Avoid language that is emotionally charged or accusatory. Lead with the business case, and once you've established that connection, introduce the social and ethical cases.

Next, be interactive. Great teachers don't just broadcast. They listen and become involved in a conversation. Spend time developing thought-provoking questions that encourage others to take a learning journey with you. The Socratic method has been around for several millennia because it works. And always make yourself available for follow-up questions or one-on-one mentoring.

Finally, give out homework. Learning isn't passive. Try to make others feel so involved that they want to go out and discover more about the subject themselves. The more they learn on their own, the more drawn in they'll be—and quite possibly, the more they'll have to teach you.

Follow Up Relentlessly

Effective evangelists are detail-oriented and accountable. These traits send a signal that you are serious and will not go away until you convince others to change.

First, keep your promises. When you're evangelizing, your students will often challenge you to provide more information. Get back to them with the promised data as quickly as possible. The sooner you follow up on your promises, the more they will believe you are serious and will listen to you.

Next, report progress. This step is especially important if you're evangelizing to a group of people about an initiative you're already undertaking. Let them know what's transpired since your initial discussion. Measure and express your progress in objective terms. Your diligence in reporting can help bring your biggest skeptics into the fold.

Finally, celebrate success. To keep others involved over the long haul, recognize their contributions publicly. Send congratulatory e-mails and post on the intranet discussion boards. Create an event or leverage an existing one and invite a wide audience. Celebrations send a signal that you are leading a winning team, making it more appealing to those not yet converted.

Welcome Your Skeptics into the Fold When They Eventually Convert
Regardless of how difficult others have made it for you to succeed, you now acknowledge them as partners. Every saver I've interviewed told me that they faced doubters who, bearing blank stares and folded arms, disagreed with the facts presented and accused them of stridency or idealism. Sometimes such skeptics even attempt to undermine your work through counterevangelism, attacking you personally.

Later, when they come around, be large enough to welcome them. Skeptics can become the most passionate converts. Many of the most significant movements are led by those who admit they were once in the dark but now see the light.

Don Ostler is a saver soldier who used these three rules effectively to evangelize a controversial idea. The delivery operations manager at Green Mountain Coffee Roasters, Ostler oversees twenty-four trucks driven by forty-eight drivers covering four warehouses around the country.

Concerned about global warming, Ostler realized that transportation was a primary driver of Green Mountain Coffee Roasters' carbon footprint, so he decided to try to cut transportation-related emissions.

In 2004, Ostler started experimenting with mixing traditional and nontraditional fuels, as well as placing nose cones on the front of his trucks to reduce wind drag. None of these efforts moved the needle, but the process educated him on the different variables that determine fuel efficiency. As he pored over fuel data, he stumbled upon the culprit that generated most of his fleet's eco-waste: engine idling during deliveries and pickups. This one factor accounted for 30 percent of all gasoline used by his fleet.

Ostler also realized that his drivers tended to leave their trucks running the entire day, even as they loaded and unloaded trucks during delivery stops. Drivers believed that idling preserved comfortable temperatures in the cabin, and that repeatedly turning an engine on and off could damage it.

Because Ostler knew these beliefs were long-standing, he couldn't simply mandate change. If the drivers didn't believe in an idle-reduction policy, they'd ignore it. Instead, Ostler decided to educate the drivers through a curriculum of presentations, events, and progress reports.

So Ostler kicked off the company's 2005 annual drivers' meeting with a fifteen-minute PowerPoint presentation that offered up a few facts, including how much fuel idling wasted, how much money that cost, and what it all meant to the company's bottom line.

Next, he asked drivers to explain why they idled during deliveries. They told him what he already knew: climate control and engine wear. He responded by giving several of them a homework assignment: Try turning off the engines and testing climate preservation.

Ostler promised that, in the meantime, his maintenance group would research the issue of whether turning off the engine created wear and tear.

Most of the crowd was visibly skeptical. But over the next few months, drivers discovered that their cabins stayed cool or hot long after they'd turned the engine off. Meanwhile, Ostler's maintenance crew found evidence that idling ran an engine hotter than normal and contributed to its wear and tear in the long run.

Ostler presented his ongoing findings at quarterly warehouse luncheons, during which he told drivers that while there might not be any individual savings here, he was concerned about the big picture. The company should do its part to help the planet because the planet needs help. This is what the company stood for, and so should the drivers.

Ostler convinced several drivers to turn their engines off during deliveries. But he still had skeptics, so he knew his job wasn't done.

Ostler's presentation at the next meeting focused on the accomplishments of a handful of drivers in that first year. Then he created a scorecard system that helped each driver measure his own idle time and fuel efficiency. One man, a vocal naysayer from the beginning, was so impressed with these accomplishments that he converted and soon became one of the no-idling movement's leaders inside the company.

During 2006, the idle-reduction program helped save the company 5,000 gallons of gasoline. Idling dropped from 30 percent of engine running time to less than 10 percent. Ostler was so proud of his team's accomplishments that he created and distributed T-shirts saying, "GMCR Saved 5,000 Gallons of Gas Annually with Idle Reduction, and I Helped."

The joke at the company is that the drivers have so bought into this program that they now shut off their engines at a long stoplight.

Once he knew this program had worked, Ostler took up a new cause, evangelizing bio-diesel fuel to business managers at the company. Over time, he has helped enhance Green Mountain Coffee Roasters' image as a sustainable company, adding to its long-standing reputation as a fair-trade advocate. Through their persistent efforts, Ostler and the rest of his Green Mountain evangelists helped the company finish at the top of *Business Ethics* magazine's 2006 Top Corporate Citizens list.

2. Unleash the Power of Many

Another way to influence others is to organize diverse groups of like-minded people inside your company. Such groups not only show senior management that there is a collective will for change, but also can penetrate corporate boundaries and spread ideas, regardless of how sprawling and massive the company might be.

A variety of different approaches exist to create and manage groups. The two most effective are to build a movement and to create a network.

Build a Movement

Movements can effect great change. Throughout history, they have caused governments to fall, wars to end, and policies to shift. Movements can start with as few as two people, and they can accomplish more with fewer people than you might imagine.

Movements are created when people come together to pursue a shared vision and/or passion. To foster a movement, find your kindred spirits at the company. You'll draw them out by being public about your beliefs. Make your vision part of your conversation at breaks, off-site meetings, and social gatherings.

Grow your group faster by advertising for new members. Post notices and send e-mails about your involvement in your socially responsible quest, and mention that you're looking for others to join in.

Next, take advantage of available corporate resources. It's much easier to start a movement around an existing corporate initiative that already has some degree of funding and support. But if you do have to start from scratch, search out existing corporate resources. Does your company give you the right to use meeting rooms and facilities, or to take time off to pursue social projects? Is the corporate intranet useful? Are marketing resources available to promote activities?

Finally, make the team you assemble highly visible. Effective movements aren't secret but very public. Look for opportunities to demonstrate the commitment, size, and/or power of your movement. Let people know this is a sizable group that's not going away.

Here's a good example from CIBC, a national bank in Canada. In 1997, the community relations group of the Edmonton, Alberta, branch signed on to sponsor the Canadian Breast Cancer Foundation's annual Run for the Cure fund-raiser. The sponsorship program offered a modest amount of financial support and encouraged CIBC employees to participate either by running in the event or pledging money to those who did. The program received a pleasant reception but was not deemed strategic to the company's core interests.

For the next three years, hundreds of tellers from Edmonton to Toronto—mostly women—signed up to run for the fund-raiser. They organized individual teams at each of the bank branch locations to strategize how to increase participation and raise more money. They took advantage of available corporate resources and participated in corporate promotions, putting up posters and wearing T-shirts and pink ribbons provided by the Canadian Breast Cancer Foundation. They talked up the fund-raiser to coworkers, friends, and family. Involvement became a point of pride.

By 2001, with thousands of CIBC employees now program participants, the fund-raiser was a major source of job satisfaction. Bank executives asked the brand-marketing group to research the impact of the company's sponsorship; the resulting data suggested that it was driving the bank's popularity with customers, especially women, and that a side benefit was a boost in employee retention.

Because of these efforts and their results, bank executives reclassified the Run for the Cure sponsorship program as strategic to the company and moved it from the community affairs department to the powerful and well-funded brand marketing group, which upped the ante by approving an additional $3 million in sponsorship money to promote the event through television, print, and Web advertisements. In 2001, approximately $10 million was raised for the Run for the Cure.

By the following year, more than 140,000 people participated in the program, due largely to CIBC advertising. Later that year, when new management took over the bank, they continued the support. Today the Run for the Cure is the largest breast-cancer fund-raising event in North America, all because a few hundred passionate tellers decided to use the workplace to organize an event about which they truly cared.

Create a Network

In many cases, the obstacle to creating change isn't people, but the structure of your organization. Companies with assorted businesses often operate as if each business unit were an independent company with its own rules, policies, and culture.

To protect their independence, business-unit leaders typically create corporate silos, a term borrowed from the military to describe organizational structures and cultural practices designed to block intervention from so-called outsiders that could upset the status quo.

These silos make it difficult to promote a cause across a company. But you can succeed by creating a network of people who operate inside each silo so that your ideas cross political and organizational boundaries.

Even if you work at a company without silos, you may need to create a vast network of kindred spirits. In my first book, *Love Is the*

KillerApp, I argued that your network is equivalent to your net worth; this is particularly true for social innovators.

Creating a network for change requires three steps. First, you have to find people who possess three qualities: common values, which means they have a passion for the issue or innovation; capabilities, which means they bring value to the table (whether it's decision-making power, innovative skills, or influence); and coverage, meaning that they provide needed representation, so your efforts will affect the whole company rather than just one business unit or regional location.

Second, once you've located your people, you'll need to link them to one another so the network can grow and produce results. If possible, connect people face-to-face, helping establish rapport among network members.

When introducing two network nodes to each other, identify their common interests and shared values ahead of time so you'll be prepared to explain the specific value each brings to the other, creating mutual interest.

Third, focus on producing companywide results. A network needs leadership, and as its creator, you provide it. Establish and communicate aspirational, yet realistic, goals. Make sure the goal is measurable and related to the business. Give each goal a due date.

Joan Krajewski, an exemplary network creator, has always been on a mission to help preserve the planet for future generations. How she might actually do so occurred to her while she was in law school and working part-time at the National Resources Defense Council. She decided that her best shot at making a difference would come from helping companies measure and improve their environmental performance.

The arena so interested Krajewski that in the mid-1990s she left her law practice for a position at American Airlines, where she helped implement an environmental management system (EMS) that measured the company's impact on the planet.

In 2005, Krajewski was approached by Microsoft, which did not have an EMS in place, to become the director of environmental policy of its hardware business unit. Shortly after arriving, Krajewski realized that Microsoft's silo organization would make the installation of a companywide EMS difficult, so she decided her best bet was to create a cross-company network of eco-minded employees.

Her first action was to recruit participants throughout the computer hardware business unit. Then, a few months later, she fanned out, meeting with other business units, such as the software applications group that made Microsoft's Office and Enterprise product lines.

Krajewski next hosted meetings throughout the company to teach others about Microsoft's environmentally related legal risks, allowing her a chance to connect with kindred spirits she might otherwise have never met.

Krajewski, who used these meetings to identify those who had a real passion for environmental sustainability, started out by asking, "What's the biggest environmental problem at Microsoft?" She followed up with each person who spoke, creating a network database of names.

She then staged cross-company educational events to discuss sustainability and environmental impact, making sure to introduce speakers to each other. For example, she would introduce Paul from the software group to Pam from the MSN Internet group, saying, "You two should get together because Paul has information that you need, Pam; and Pam, you have technology that can help Paul meet his goals in product sustainability."

She also took advantage of corporate resources, including Microsoft technology tools such as SharePoint, which permits people to share PowerPoint presentations, and LiveMeeting, which allows dozens or even hundreds of people to participate in a live video-based chat.

Once Krajewski had connected people, she focused them on creating results by establishing urgency around environmental issues. She presented data that showed why Microsoft had to be ready for upcoming regulations and carbon-emissions taxes, because otherwise the company could face dramatic financial setbacks. From a branding standpoint, she illustrated how Microsoft would have to be the greenest company in the technology business to maintain its position as an industry leader. She also coordinated the people in her network by issuing ambitious goals to each group, such as establishing a company-wide environmental-management system and reducing the packaging size across product lines by more than 50 percent.

In two years, using this find-connect-focus strategy, Krajewski had built an extensive network of saver soldiers representing all business units at Microsoft who were able to create an EMS and implement it companywide. With the data center group, Krajewski also collaborated with developers to build a software tool that measures carbon emissions on a daily basis; initially for internal use, it's now available for purchase by any company.

Network members also created widely distributed white papers on the business benefits of reducing or eliminating packaging. Inside the hardware group, product designers reduced packaging of products such as the Xbox gaming console by as much as 40 percent; in the software group, network members also innovated how products were packaged, reducing waste and carbon emissions dramatically.

In the end, Krajewski turned what could have been an obstacle—the company's size—into a resource. She used the depth of the employee pool to find coworkers who cared about the environment to create an effective network. Rather than seeing a scarcity of opportunities, Krajewski took the abundance view, believing that the power of many can accomplish anything.

3. Mentor Your Leaders

No matter how persuasive you can be, how committed you are, or how many peers you sign up, there are going to be times when real change will require your leaders to become as involved as you are.

What do you do when a business revolution is under way and your leadership doesn't realize it? You find an opportunity to become a reverse mentor. Reverse mentoring takes place when you help someone above you in the organizational chart understand new concepts in business.

During the 1990s Internet Revolution, a great deal of reverse mentoring took place—young, Internet-savvy workers, sometimes sporting nose rings and spiked purple hair, were invited into executives' corner offices to show them how this new thing called the World Wide Web worked. At the time, many business leaders were fearful that their inability to understand the Net was going to ruin their business. They needed help, they asked for it, they got it.

People often made fun of this kind of mentoring, and several national advertisements for tech-related companies featured strange-looking twentysomethings taking older corporate execs under their wings. But in the twenty-first century, reverse mentoring is becoming common. Today's leaders, who realize they must stay on top of emerging business trends, know that their frontline employees and managers often have a better understanding of the marketplace than they do.

Odds are good that if you have something intelligent to say and the courage to say it, you're going to be listened to, and perhaps even asked to continue the conversation. As I said previously, business surveys report that about eight out of ten CEOs prioritize corporate social-responsibility efforts on their strategic agendas. As long as you are smart about how you convey your ideas, they're likely to respond positively.

Here are five steps that will help you communicate more effectively.

First, make sure you find the right place and time to initiate mentorship. If you approach your executives randomly, you risk being misunderstood or, worse, being perceived as insubordinate. The convergence you seek combines a pressing business issue with a realistic window of opportunity—for example, perhaps you know of an upcoming corporate meeting where you'll have a chance to take the platform, or an event where questions are encouraged.

One particularly good opportunity occurs when customers demand that your company catch up with the times. At Interface, customers were asking hard questions about the company's treatment of the environment. Joyce LaValle used that fact to reach out to her CEO.

Second, make the company's success the focus of your initial counseling. Harking back to the Law of the Ledger, place the baby—the company—in the middle of the table as you advise your leader. Focus your comments on helping the company survive and/or thrive. Don't make it sound as though you're simply helping your leaders catch up with the times or improve themselves as professionals: That approach is too emotionally charged. Keep yourself focused on the business case.

Third, connect with your leader's heart. It's important to talk business, but you also need to engage your leaders at a higher level so they'll have the courage to climb out of the ninety-day box and make

a long-term commitment; this is especially true if they face potential opposition from their board or other leaders outside the mentorship loop.

When applicable, connect with your company's (or its founders')
values that support your mentorship. For example, if your company's founder supported the environment, remind your leaders of
that. The same is true if stated values include employee development, partner ethics, and so on. By connecting with the company's
time-honored principles, you can talk about issues softer than cold
hard cash, further motivating your leader to do the right thing.

Fourth, be supportive, not combative. You may have strong feelings, and you may even be 100 percent right, but showing anger or
frustration during the process will get you nowhere except, perhaps,
out the door.

Finally, stick with the program. Mentorship is not a single event.
Education takes time. Make yourself available for one-on-one ses-
sions, and be willing to take on homework assignments, even if they
require personal time to complete. Always be patient, particularly if
your leader is slow to come around.

Sometimes this type of mentoring program can effect a powerful
and unlikely outcome. Here's an example:

Louise Young is a software-quality manager at defense contrac-
tor Raytheon. In the summer of 2001, she was invited to present
at Raytheon's first diversity forum, a gathering of four hundred
leaders.

Openly gay at work for many years, Young had founded and led
Raytheon's Gay, Lesbian, Bisexual, and Transgender Alliance; the
company was now asking her to talk about the group's contribution
to corporate productivity.

At the time, Raytheon didn't offer domestic-partner benefits,
although Young had been pushing for them. According to Bill Swan-

son, then senior vice president, Raytheon executives were split on the issue; many, including CEO Daniel Burnham, felt there was no pressing business reason to offer them.

The climate for gays at Raytheon was poor; few were open about their identity for fear of being passed over for promotions or plum assignments. "I had to seize this moment or it would be gone forever," Young says. "Getting domestic-partner benefits approved was an outside hope. What I really wanted to do was just get our leadership to walk a mile in our shoes."

On May 23, 2001, Young made her presentation during a panel discussion, beginning her remarks with the following statement: "I'm here to discuss productivity in the context of being free from distraction."

She next offered up a simple productivity formula: "Using GLBT employees as an example, we can very reasonably expect that about 5 percent of the workforce at Raytheon is gay/lesbian, bisexual, or transgender. Let's say that in that 5 percent of the workforce, there were distractions that caused a 10 percent productivity loss. And let's assume a figure like an average annual salary of, say, $50,000. If you add those together, that yields a $25 million price tag for distractions in the workplace."

Several people in the audience whistled at the number.

Young then explained what these distractions were, from fear of job loss and harassment to loneliness and discomfort.

"Let me give you an example," she said. "I want you to imagine going back after this conference to your office or your cubicle and removing all symbols of your personal life. Take down the pictures of your family. Take off your wedding ring. Never, ever mention your family or your personal life in any type of conversation at work. And if you slip, cover it quickly, because you might lose your job or a chance at a promotion."

She paused to let the audience think. "Now," she continued, "if you can't bring 100 percent of yourself to work, how can you give 100 percent of yourself back to Raytheon?"

Young remembers staring out into the audience and seeing men glance at their left hand, then back at her, and gulp. She could feel the change in attitude, but for the unaffected, she said, "We must adhere to our Raytheon core values, the ones we talk about all the time: respecting one another, fostering teamwork, and collaboration."

Young next explained why domestic-partner benefits would send a clear signal to gay and lesbian employees that they were included in the company family, and told the audience that she would be happy to mentor anyone who wanted to know more. She then closed by letting everyone know how proud she was of the company for creating this forum.

The reaction was swift and significant. Swanson signed on to be one of her mentees, as did other leaders who contacted her with questions, to which Young replied with concrete tips. And several executives who had opposed domestic-partner benefits morphed into its evangelists. "We had one ex–military executive at that forum," Swanson says, "who had been against domestic-partner benefits from the beginning and was vocal about it. Young changed his thinking and he became a supporter."

In late 2001, Raytheon's leadership unanimously adopted a liberal domestic-partner benefits policy. Not limited to health care coverage, it included domestic-partner relocation subsidies, pension dispersal to the partner, and health club memberships. By the next year, Raytheon's two key competitors, Lockheed Martin and Northrop Grumman, had followed, adding domestic-partner benefits to their employee benefits package.

In 2003, Swanson was promoted to CEO; later that year, he was voted the company's chairman. As such, he quickly elevated diversity to the top of the corporate agenda. In 2005, the Human Rights Coalition, one of the largest gay and lesbian rights advocacy organizations, gave Raytheon a perfect 100 on its Corporate Equality Index, the first defense company ever to receive such a score. And in 2007, the U.S. Department of Labor presented its annual diversity award to Raytheon, the first time a pure defense firm had ever won the honor.

"Young is my hero," Swanson says, "because she got out of her comfort zone. She cared about the company, not just her personal interests. I knew we had to get it right or we'd never be a great company—we wouldn't be able to recruit top candidates in the future."

Young was a software-quality manager who led a handful of reports. Yet, in one meeting, she jumped multiple rungs up the corporate ladder and helped change the face of Raytheon and the defense industry. Now that's a saver soldier.

14

Good Gravy: The Power of Being a Saver Soldier

After I gave a talk about the Responsibility Revolution at a leadership convention in Washington, D.C., Ron Merriman, a financial services manager at a local bank, joined my table for dinner. He quickly told me that he was intrigued by my speech, but I could tell from his body language that he had doubts.

Sure enough, as dessert arrived, a torrent of questions emerged: "What will it really cost to follow your advice? What if the revolution takes years to make its way to my industry? Why shouldn't I spend my precious resources working on new products or marketing schemes?"

These questions, all fair, came down to this: "What is the cost for my company, and for me, to become a saver soldier?"

Pulling my chair closer to Ron's, I told him that in the long run, social responsibility can be achieved at no cost to people or companies. Good, smart companies succeed. If you always connect your business to your social innovations, and you follow the six laws of the saver soldier, you cannot hurt your company by helping it do good. Strategic social responsibility is excellent for business, which is why Patagonia, SAS Institute, Aveda, Whole Foods, and many other early adopters flourished even before the revolution was under way.

Doing good may actually be the very best way to succeed. As proof, I cited a 2000 study from research company Towers Perrin that examined the financial returns of twenty-five companies that excelled in taking care of their stakeholders. In the fifteen years from 1984 to 1999, these companies outperformed the S&P 500 index by more than 126 percent.

Ron was impressed, but wondered if perhaps this was just a coincidence. I told him that I'd had a similar response when I first read the study, so I uncovered more proof—a study done at the Haas School of Business at the University of California, Berkeley, that also looked at whether doing good led to doing well. Examining multiyear data for almost all of the companies on the S&P 500, its analysis confirmed that a statistically significant relationship existed between socially responsible business and solid financial performance.

Why did these companies outperform their competitors? Ron asked.

There are many reasons, I replied, but the primary one may well be the virtuous-circle effect. As mentioned in the "Save Your Communities" section, stakeholders give back to the companies that take care of them.

I also explained that companies that don't adhere to the virtuous circle create a vicious cycle instead. They take and take and take from their business ecosystem until there's almost nothing left. They are parasites of, rather than partners with, their stakeholders. Eventually, most stakeholders will turn against such a company and conduct business with it only for strong, immediate reasons, such as low price or convenience. Worse, these stakeholders will be quick to sue, boycott, or ignore the company's products when displeased. Eventually, when the company's products or services are no longer well priced or convenient, the stakeholders will flee, as they did from Enron and WorldCom.

As for Ron himself, I said this: "Let me offer you a promise. If you help your company make a positive difference in the world, you'll feel your work has meaning, and you'll take pride in knowing that you're contributing to something larger than yourself."

That promise applies to every reader of this book, as well.

Then I told Ron a story I heard from Interface CEO Ray Anderson:

In 1997, Interface hosted a group of clients for a show-and-tell meeting inside its warehouse factory so that Anderson and his executive team could evangelize the Interface way.

One of the attendees, a senior manager at one of Interface's biggest clients, was a vocal skeptic, and she made that fact clear throughout the gathering. Then, during a break, she excused herself to go to the ladies' room, which meant having to walk through the factory.

Along the way, she encountered a forklift driver hauling a huge roll of carpet and singing to himself. When he stopped his truck to let her pass, she asked, "What are you so happy about?"

"My job!" he replied.

"And what vocation is that?" she asked.

"Ma'am," he said, "I come to work every day to help save the earth. That's what I do for a living."

Stunned by his enthusiasm, she quizzed him for a few minutes. He reiterated his happiness and then added, "Ma'am, I don't want to be rude, but if I don't get this roll of carpet to that machine over there in time, our waste figures will go out of sight. We could miss our carbon-emissions figures for the week. That's unacceptable."

The woman returned to the meeting a changed person. Now she understood what Interface was doing—driving up quality and profits at the same time. "There's something your people have," she told Anderson. "Not just for their jobs, but for this company. I would call it love."

From that moment on, the woman became a sustainability convert. "Why aren't we doing the same thing as Interface?" she asked her own people. "Why isn't everyone in the world doing the same thing? Let's go back to the office and get started up the road to Mount Sustainability."

15

If Not You, Then Who?

Before closing this book, bear with me for a moment as we go back in time to America in 1763. England's King George III, facing mounting debts from the French and Indian Wars, had just decided to tax the American colonies. Britain then passed both the Stamp Act and the Townsend Acts, levying taxes on a variety of British products, including tea, paper, paint, and metals.

Enraged, the colonists responded by protesting taxation without representation in the English government. Among these early revolutionaries was a highly influential group called the Sons of Liberty, which began forming chapters in every colony, meeting secretly to discuss ways to protest British taxation. Some members went further, raising the idea of independence.

One of the Sons of Liberty's first acts was to organize a boycott against British tea. John Hancock, who later became the first person to sign the Declaration of Independence, and other prominent revolutionaries took the boycott a step further by importing tea from Holland and selling it directly to the colonists. This strategy led to a 90 percent drop in sales revenues for the British East India company, which had held a virtual tea monopoly on colonial tea, pushing it to the brink of bankruptcy.

Company lobbyists pushed back, pressuring Parliament for help, which came in the form of the 1773 Tea Act, making British East India tax-exempt and allowing it to sell tea in the colonies for half its original price.

Colonists were now more infuriated, viewing this act as an overt attempt to give British East India an unfair trade advantage.

One such colonist was Samuel Adams Jr., a former tax collector in Boston. Adams, a local leader of the Sons of Liberty, started organizing rallies at Boston Harbor to protest British East India's tax exemption. Openly railing against the crown, Adams stirred up large crowds with talk of independence.

The protests unnerved the captain, owner, and crew of the *Dartmouth* and two other ships bearing British East India tea that had recently docked in Boston Harbor. They were about to return to Britain until Massachusetts governor Thomas Hutchinson stepped in, ordering the harbor blocked and the tea to be unloaded and put on sale.

The *Dartmouth*'s captain delivered the news to Adams, who was at that moment leading an 8,000-person rally at Boston's Griffith's Wharf. Adams in turn related the news to the mob, declaring, "This meeting can do nothing more to save the country. . . . If we retreat now, everything we have done becomes useless. If Hutchinson will not send tea back to England, perhaps we can brew a pot of it especially for him!"

The crowd whooped its approval, and leaders of the Sons of Liberty hatched a plan, putting the word out to all its members.

Later that night, 150 Sons of Liberty, thinly disguised as Indians, boarded the three ships, unloading more than 90,000 pounds of tea, breaking open the containers, and dumping them into Boston Harbor. News of this Boston Tea Party quickly spread throughout the colonies, inspiring other acts of protest.

The British government promptly closed the harbor and declared Adams, Hancock, and other Sons of Liberty guilty of high treason. Soon, Redcoats were marching, Paul Revere was riding, and the American Revolution was under way.

But what would have happened if no one had shown up at the Boston Tea Party? What if the revolutionaries had thought, "I don't feel like going—let someone else take the risk"?

This is the question I now ask you: If you don't show up for the Responsibility Revolution at work, who will?

Revolution is in the air. ThemGeners are organizing against just-for-profit business and they are willing to sacrifice to change it. Even if your CEO is already aware of this news, and he or she likely is, no CEO can do the heavy lifting alone. So if *you* don't show up, you and your company may wind up on the wrong side of the revolution.

Let me ask a final question: If not now, then when? The Responsibility Revolution is already under way. The longer you wait to join it, the more likely you and your company will struggle to play catch-up or miss out on opportunities to gain an unshakable edge over your laggard competitors.

If Joyce LaValle waited to send Ray Anderson *The Ecology of Commerce*, how many million pounds of carpet would be sitting in landfills right now? If executives at UPS had waited to bring its School-to-Work program to Louisville, how many kids would have failed to graduate from local high schools?

Why not make today the day you become a saver soldier? Your lack of action now could result in a terrible series of lost opportunities.

A few years ago, I gave a lecture at a technology conference about the dangerous high-tech/low-touch management style in which e-mail replaces face-to-face contact, even when the manager's employees work in the same building.

It's possible, I argued, that you could work for months without much real human contact with your coworkers or your boss. I explained how dangerous this isolation can be when coupled with a lack of recognition—too many managers fear that if they give specific praise to an employee who is later laid off, the compliment could fuel an employee lawsuit for unjust dismissal.

This pattern leads to workplace depression, I continued, presenting research showing how depression in turn leads to ill health, poor productivity, and low morale. I argued that everyone in the audience needed to rescue their people from such unnecessary pain and suffering, and that that task was a vital component of good management and saving the world at work.

I concluded my talk with this thought: "If there are people in your life who are important to you, and you haven't given them sufficient recognition in the last three months, shame on you. If you've reduced your relationships to e-mail threads, shame on you. If you acted like this toward your children, I would tell you that you were not a good parent. If you did this to your friends, I would tell you you're not a good friend. If this is your management style, I would tell you you're not a good manager."

Then I invited the audience to ask me questions or share stories.

A few days later, I received an e-mail from someone I'll call Steve, a manager at a software company. In the note he admitted, "I'm guilty as charged. I'm exactly the type of manager you described. I have nine software engineers who report to me. We all work in the same building, and I've seen only one of them face-to-face in at least three months. We do everything over e-mail and instant messenger.

"Worse than that, I haven't praised anyone since last year's annual review. Yet all nine of my engineers are great workers and good people, and they don't deserve to be treated this way. What should I do?"

I told him to take immediate action by spending time thinking about the contributions each one of his nine employees made to the company, and to him. Meet with them in person, I said, and give them the recognition they deserve. The rest will take care of itself.

About a week later, Steve sent me a note I'll never forget as long as I live. The subject line of the e-mail was "Xbox Story." The following tale is somewhat graphic, but I have to tell it in full to convey its power and show why it changed my life.

Steve told me that he'd met with all nine of his engineers that day, making one positive personal and one positive professional comment.

Two days later, one of his engineers (whose real name he disguised as Lenny) entered Steve's cubicle just as Steve was arriving at work. Carrying a box wrapped in brown paper and topped with a bow, Lenny told Steve he wanted to give him a gift.

Steve unwrapped the box and found a remarkable prize: an Xbox gaming system and a copy of the John Madden Football video game. Steve was thrilled.

But it wasn't his birthday or a special occasion, and Steve hadn't given Lenny a raise for as long as he could remember. On top of that, all of his engineers had been grumbling that they could hardly make ends meet on their meager salaries. So Steve asked Lenny where he got the extra money for such a lavish gift.

Lenny looked him straight in the eye and said words no manager ever expects to hear: "I sold my chrome-plated 9mm semiautomatic."

Lenny told Steve that though he had worked at the company for two years, in all that time Steve had never asked Lenny a single question about himself. Now he wanted to answer the questions Steve had never asked.

Lenny had moved to town from Denver the day after he buried his mom, who had died suddenly. Lenny's mother was his only close friend and only real confidante. "She understood my nerdy ways," he said.

So Lenny moved to a new city and took a job at a company where he thought he would find other nerds and make new friends. But, he said, "People here aren't very friendly. No one ever speaks to me in the halls or the lunch room."

When Steve looked surprised, Lenny continued, "I've worked here two years, and if I died, you'd only find out from payroll, because the direct deposit wouldn't go in anymore. That's how disconnected I thought you were from me.

"I don't have a single friend in the company. I come in every day, log in, and spend my life looking at a computer screen."

Lenny said that his only friend in the world was the Internet. So he logged on daily to look for solutions, and found several. "Suicide chat rooms," he said. "They're filled with other people just like me. And they told me what to do. They told me about 'the program.'

"The first step is to buy a gun so beautiful that you want to come home from work every day and admire it. It helps you get over being afraid of it."

Lenny saved up for several months and bought a chrome-plated, 9mm pistol, which he stored in a Cohiba cigar box. Every night when he got home from work, he'd open the box and look at the gun.

A few months later, he started the program's next step. After work he'd put on the right mood music, which in his case was Kurt Cobain, and then get up the courage to take the gun out of the box and practice holding it in his hand.

Steve, silent, let Lenny spill his story.

"There's another step, called teething," Lenny explained. "It's a difficult but important part of the program. Here you get used to the sensation of the barrel of the gun sitting on top of your teeth, because they teach you right away in the chat room that you've got to put the gun inside your mouth and not upside your head, otherwise you'll only graze yourself and it won't work.

"And it takes a while," Lenny added, "to get over the shakes."

Another step is called "the final approach," which was where Lenny had recently arrived. "You load the gun. You take the safety off. You put the barrel of the gun inside your mouth and put some pressure on the trigger. Each night, same routine, more pressure. I was getting closer and closer and closer. I was almost there.

"And then, the other day," Lenny continued, "you freaked me out. You come into my cubicle, you put your sweaty arm around me, and you tell me that you admired the fact that I turned in every project one day early, and it helped you sleep at night. Which, by the way, Steve, is my style. You also told me that I had an incredible sense of humor over e-mail, and that I made the whole group laugh when times were stressful."

Moving closer to his boss, Lenny whispered, "But then you told me, 'Lenny, I'm glad you came into my life.'

"I went home that night, put on Kurt Cobain, and started my nightly routine. But when I opened up the cigar box, as the light reflected off the chrome, the hairs on the back of my neck stood up. And for the first time I was afraid to die. Before I could catch myself, I said out loud to no one in particular, 'Lenny, I'm glad you came into my life.'

"At that minute, I was off the program. I shut the cigar box and put it in my backpack. I called in sick yesterday, because I wanted to sell the gun immediately. I took it back to the pawnshop that sold it to me, and they gave me a few hundred bucks. I thought to myself, "What do I want to spend this money on?"

"Then I remembered that you had been bellyaching for a month over e-mail that your financial controller at home, aka your wife, wouldn't let you buy the new Xbox gaming system because you had a new baby."

With tears streaming down his cheeks, Lenny said, "Sir, in exchange for my life, my soul, this gift is for you."

Acknowledgments

This book was the result of a combined effort of dozens of people who shared my vision: Let's make a difference with this book. Let's change the world.

I can't name everyone, but here, from the bottom of my heart, I want to thank:

Don Weisberg, for more or less giving me this book as an assignment. He believes that businesses can do good in this world. More important, he believed that I was the one to craft the idea into a book.

Jan Miller, my literary agent, for all her support. Love your guts.

Heidi Krupp and the team at Krupp Kommunications, for spreading the Love and never taking *no* for an answer.

Roger Scholl, my editor at Doubleday, for his undying commitment to the reader experience

The Doubleday team, including: Steve Rubin, Michael Palgon, Beth Meister, Meredith McGinnis, Liz Hazelton, Lindsay Mergens, Rex Bonomelli, and Ellen Elchepp. Together we are bringing this message to the business world and beyond!

The research team: Elisa Vandernoot, Rebecca Ho, and William Maldridge. You went beyond the call to find the proof behind my premise.

Elaine Farris, my transcriber, for your amazing level of service and quality.

Finally, Gene Stone, my writing partner and trusted advisor: You are absolutely the heart and soul of this work, from beginning to end. BFF.

Index

A. B. Dick/IPS, 168
Abbott Labs, 137
Abramovitz, Janet, 179
Adams, Michael, 32
Adams, Samuel, Jr., 227
AIG, 28
Alloy Media, 36
American Apparel, 172–73
American Backlash (Adams), 31
American Hotel and Lodging Assn.,
   202
Anderson, Ray, 12–15, 87, 88, 104,
   110, 143, 224, 228
Arizona State University, 164
Art of the Long View, (Schwartz), 111
Atlantis Solutions, 112–13
Aveda, 46–51, 154, 222
   assessing new products, 196, 197
   hybrid lighting, 138–40
   Love Pure-Fume, 49, 197
   transportation, reducing
     footprint, 187

Ball, Diane, 141–43
Ballew, Paul, 75

Barney's, 202
Barr, Tony, 55
Barry, Daniel, 146
BASF, 87
Ben & Jerry's, 148–50
Bendell, Jem, 28
Benioff, Mark, 168
Bently Prince Street, Inc., 88
Big Pie People, 106
BMW, 111
Body Shop, The, 90
Bowling Alone (Putnam), 32
BP (British Petroleum), 67
Braungart, Michael, 138, 183
British Columbia Lottery System, 132
Broadcast.com, 45, 107–8, 128–30
Brodsky, Stuart, 193
Brokaw, Tom, 58
Bronczek, David, 165
Buckingham, Jane, 173
Buffett, Warren, 8
Burnham, Daniel, 219
Business Alliance for Local Living
   Economies (BALLE), 171
Business Ethics magazine, 37

Cadbury Schweppes, 77
Calvert Group, 40, 41, 61, 70–71,
    72, 82
Camizan, Arnaldo Neyra, 149
Canon Corporation, 102, 146–47
Carbon footprint, 203
Carbonfund.org, 189
Carbon offsets, 188–89
Carbon Trust, 77
Carbon-view.com, 199
Cary Academy, 57
Cassandra Report, 29, 173
Catmull, Ed, 191
Center for Environmental Leader-
    ship in Business, 179, 186
Cessna Aircraft Company, 172, 174
CFL (compact fluorescent light-
    bulb), 64–66, 76–77, 178
Charney, Dov, 172–73
Chesbrough, Henry, 66, 114
Chick-Fil-A, 143
Chouinard, Yvon, 52, 55, 58, 98
Christensen, Clayton, 16
CIBC, 211–12
Cisco Networks, 150, 163
Citigroup, Inc., 67, 135
City Year, 160–61
Climatecare.org, 189, 203
ClimateCare.org, 203
Cluetrain Manifesto, The (Locke
    et al.), 42
Columbia Business School, 91, 144
Communities In Schools, 57
Computers for Schools, Chicago,
    175

Computer TakeBack Campaign, 69,
    71–73
Connelly, Liam, 191
Conseil, Dominique, 50–51, 139,
    154–55
Consorta, 168–69
Conway, Bill, 21
Costco, 63, 145–46
Cost savings, 14, 26, 50
Covey, Stephen, 105
Cradle to Cradle (McDonough and
    Braungart), 138, 183
Craigslist.org, 162
Crayons to Computers, 175
Cuban, Mark, 45
Cummins Diesel, Inc., 153–54

DaimlerChrysler, 75
Danis, Peter and Laurie, 177–79
DataDepositBox.com, 189
DBM Career Services, 37
Deep Economy (McKibben), 194
Dell, Michael, 71, 72, 84
Dell, Susan, 72
Dell Computer, 69–73, 84, 143
Delnor Community Hospital,
    141–42
Deming, W. E., 19, 22
Dillon, Marty, 135–36
Dooky Chase's restaurant, 95
Douglas, Dave, 186
Dow Jones Sustainability Index
    (DJSI), 41
Dreyfus, Third Century Fund, 40
Duke, Mike, 15

Dupee, Michael, 156
DuPont, 15, 87, 128

Earth Month/Earth Day, 50
Earth Summit, 1992, 48
Eco-Advantage, 24
EcologicalMail.org, 184
Ecology of Commerce, The (Hawken),
    12, 34, 88, 228
Electro-Motive, 174–75
Elkington, John, 83
Ellison, Larry, 84
Energy BBDO, 5
Energy Star, 193, 194
Enron, 8, 28, 33, 59, 104, 223
Environmental management system
    (EMS), 213–16
Environmental Paper Network, 180
Equal Exchange, 149,153
Ernst & Young, 127
Eskew, Mike, 104
Estée Lauder, 49–51
Esty, Daniel, 26, 197
Ethical consumerism, 77
E-Trade Inc., 106
Evangelical Climate Initiative, 91
Exxon, 8

Fair Trade Certified, 156, 157
FedEx, 21, 165–66
Figlio restaurant, 177–78
Fishman, Charles, 79
Fleishman-Hillard, Inc., 126–27
Fleming, John, 64
Fletcher Allen Healthcare, 175

Florida Power & Light, 67
Ford Motor Company, 76, 91, 149
Four Seasons restaurant, 150–51
Freeman, Bennett, 61
Friedman, Milton, 31
Fujiwara, Seika, 147

Gates, Bill, 8
Gausman, Jim, 139
GE (General Electric), 59, 61, 65,
    66, 84
General Mills mentoring program,
    127
*General Theory of Employment,
    Interest and Money, The*
    (Keynes), 170
Gifford, Kathie Lee, 155
Global Greengrants Fund, 50
Glover, Darren, 30–31
GM (General Motors), 10, 74,
    111, 147
Good Earthkeeping program, 202
Goodnight, Jim, 55–57, 66, 109
Google, 54, 57, 66–67, 84, 144,
    188, 192
Gore, Al, 28
Graham, John, 127
Great Depression, 6, 7
Green Gospel, 91–92
Green Mountain Coffee Roasters,
    156–57, 191, 207–9
GreenPDF.com, 184
Green Press Initiative, 36
Green to Gold (Esty and Winston),
    26, 197

Grocery stores, 202
Gupta, Ashok, 64

H&R Block, 133–34
Habitat for Humanity, 142
Hallmark Compassionate
    Connections, 127
Hamburg, Steve, 64–65
Hamel, Gary, 18
Hancock, John, 226
Hawken, Paul, 12, 34, 188
Health South, 28
Heartmath Institute, 139, 141–42
Hedwig, Jane, 55
Herman Miller, Inc., 138
Hewlett-Packard, 144, 198
Home Depot, 64
Honeywell Corporation, 80–81, 87
Houston, Texas, 104
Hunter, Joel, 91

IBM, 144
IKEA, 26–27, 57, 197
Immelt, Jeffrey, 59–61, 65, 98
Inconvenient Truth, An (film), 28
Industrial Revolution, 17
ING Direct, 108
Innovator's Dilemma, The
    (Christensen), 16
In Style, 51
Intel, 128
Interdependence, 103
Interface, Inc., 10, 12–15, 87–89, 97,
    124, 178, 194, 195, 217

Jackson, Rick, 129
Japan
    Quality Revolution and, 19–23, 67
    Shuchu Kiyaku, 146–47
Jennings, Jason, 27
Jubb, Jim, 65

Kaku, Ryuzaburo, 102
Kasiarz, David, 141
Kay, Alan, 99
Keynes, John Maynard, 170
Khazei, Alan, 160
Koogle, Tim, 119
Krajewski, Joan, 201, 213–16
Krumsiek, Barbara, 82
Kyosei, 102
Kyoto Protocol, 87

La Minita Tarrazu, Costa Rica, 156
Larry's Market, Seattle, 175
Lauder, Leonard, 49
LaValle, Joyce, 12, 13–14, 15, 88, 97,
    98–99, 124, 217, 228
LaValle, Melissa, 12, 15
La Villa restaurant, 167
Leading the Revolution (Hamel), 18
Lencioni, Patrick, 136
Lennox Hotel, Boston, 201–2
Letterman, Elmer, 150–51
Levine, Rick, 42
Lewis, Jessica, 166–67
Lifeworth, 28
LiveVault.com, 189
Locke, Christopher, 42

Lockheed Martin, 220
LOHAS, 35–36
Louisville, Kentucky, 103–4, 164, 228
Love Is the Killer App (Sanders), 212–13
Lovins, Amory, 189
Lush Fresh Handmade Cosmetics, 10

MacArthur, Gen. Douglas, 19
Malcolm Baldrige Award, 21
Mannix, Elizabeth, 144
Marcus, Stanley, Jr., 101–2, 103
Margolis, Paul, 112
Marks & Spencer, 77
Martin, Roger, 33
Maslow, Abraham, 7
Master Manufacturing, 155
Masters of Networking (Misner), 151
Mattel, Inc., 148
Mattoon, Ashley, 179
McCormick, Ron, 64
McDonough, William, 138, 183, 201
McKinsey & Co., 6, 78
Medtronic, 10
Merck & Co., 28
Merriman, Ron, 222–24
Metafacts, 140
Metropolitan College, 104
Meyer, Russ, 172
Microsoft, 144, 198–99, 201, 213–16
Mid-Course Correction (Anderson), 15
Middlebury College, 194–95
Millard, Lisa, 133–34

Milliken Carpet, 87, 88
Misner, Ivan, 151
Mohawk Carpet, 87, 88
Montgomery, David, 38
Morgan, Robert, 38
Mortgage industry, 7
Motorola, 20, 67, 119
Munger, Tolles & Olson, 163

Nashua Corporation, 21
Nathan, Pat, 72
National Carpeting Recycling Agreement, 87
National Labor Committee, 155
National Minority Supplier Development Council, 154
Natural Resource Defense Council, 64
Neale, Margaret, 144
Neiman Marcus, 100–101
Net Impact, 37
New Economics Foundation, 169
Ning, Ted, 77
Nissan, 146–47
Nokia, 23
Northland Church, Longwood, Florida, 91
Northrop Grumman, 220
Northwestern Kellogg School, 91

Oak Ridge National Labs, 139
Office Depot, 153–54
"1 Percent for the Planet Alliance," 54
Oracle, 84

Oregon legislature, 9
Ostler, Don, 207–9

P&L (profit and loss) new criteria, 26
Paper Cuts (Abramovitz and
    Mattoon), 179
Parker, Rod, 175
Patagonia, Inc., 52–55, 191, 222
    "The 1 Percent Solution," 53
Pax World Fund, 40, 41
Penn State University Web
    calculator, 122
Pepsi Bottling Group, 38, 140, 141
PepsiCo, 77
Peters, Tom, 115
Phish, 175
Phoenix International Raceway,
    164–65
Porter, Michael, 164
Poulter, Devin, 151–52
PRI (Principles for Responsible
    Investment), 83
Project 50, The (Peters), 115
Project Planet Corporation, 202
PSPs (personal sustainability
    projects), 192
Purpose Driven Life, The (Warren), 91
Putnam, Robert, 32

Quality Revolution, 19–24, 67, 119,
    146–47, 152

Ralph's markets, 202
Ramus, Catherine, 38
Rare, consulting company, 50

Ray, Paul H., 35
Raytheon, 218–21
Real, Terrance, 139
Rechelbacher, Horst, 46–51, 98, 196
Responsibility Revolution, 25
    accepting call to action, 226–28
    acting to improve social value and
        employees, 125–44
    acting to improve social value and
        vendors, 144–58
    acting to influence others, 204–21
    acting to save communities, 159–
        76
    acting to save the planet, 177–203
    change in circumstances phase,
        23–28
    disruption phase, 68–85
    innovators phase, 10, 44–67
Revere, Paul, 230
Rheingold, Howard, 7
Ricoh, 69
Royal Dutch/Shell, 111
Rubinfield, Iris, 154

Safe Kids Worldwide, 164
Safeway, 84
Salesforce.com, 54, 168–69
Sall, John, 55–57
Sam's Club, 146
Sanders Group hotels, 201–2
Sara Lee Corporation, 158
Sarbanes-Oxley bill, 8–9
SAS Institute, 10, 55–57, 66, 109,
    142–43, 188, 222
Saver soldiers, 97–100, 104, 168, 221

Schneider, Robin, 70, 72–73
Schwab, Charles M., 131–34
Schwartz, Peter, 111, 112
Scott, Lee, 61–64, 167
Searls, Don, 42
"Sharesm," 9
Shaw Carpet, 87, 88
Shuchu Kiyaku, 147
Silveri, Tom, 37
Simms, Andrew, 169–70
Sinegal, Jim, 145–46
Skozelas, Patricia, 202
Smith, Adam, 109
Smith, Fred, 21
Socially responsible investing (SRI),
    39–40
Softward Spectrum, 151, 152
Sony, 146, 148
Sperber, Bryan, 164–65
Speth, James Gustave, 33
Spherion Corporation, 38
Starbucks, 38, 67
Steelcase, Inc., 140
Stiller, Bob, 156
Strong, John, 168–69
Suminokura, Soan, 146
Sun Microsystems, 127, 186
Supply Chain Consulting, 198
Swanson, Bill, 218–19, 220–21
Swartz, Jeffrey, 160
Sylvania, 65

Table Group, The, 136
Texas Campaign for the Environ
    ment, 70

Texas Instruments, 194
TheGreenOffice.com, 189
Theory of Moral Sentiments, The
    (Smith), 109
Third Wave, 106–7
3M Corporation, 21
Three Signs of a Miserable Job, The
    (Lencioni), 136
Timberland Company, 10, 95–97,
    159–61, 191, 192
Time, 51, 199
Toffler, Alvin, 107–8
Totten, Michael, 179
Toyota, 73–75, 171
    hybrid cars (Prius), 67, 73–74, 111
Trader Joe's, 202
TransFair USA, 157
Triple bottom line, 83–84
Turner, Pat, 187

UCLA Environmental Coalition,
    157–58
Unilever, 150–52
United Airlines, 121
United Center, Chicago, 175
United Nations PRI, 83
United Way, 168
UPS, 103–4, 163, 228

Wack, Pierre, 111
Wal-Mart, 8, 63–66, 76–77, 80, 121,
    145–46, 155, 166–67
War for Talent, The (McKinsey &
    Co.), 6, 78
Warren, Rick, 91

Washington Area Gleaning Network, 175

Waveland, Mississippi, 166–67

Weatherup, Craig, 37

Weinberger, David, 42

Welch, Jack, 59

Wellness programs, 140–42

Werbach, Adam, 192

West Michigan Business Forum, 197

Wheaton Plastics (now ALCAN), 50

Whitener, Gordon, 13

Whole Foods, 10, 64, 84, 222

Wild Oats, 64

Winfrey, Oprah, 57

Winston, Andrew, 26, 197

Women's Business Enterprise National Council, 154

"Working Relations" (Planned Perspectives), 147

WorldCom, 8, 28, 33, 59, 223

World Commission on Environment and Development, 190

Wright, Tom, 141–42

Wyndham Hotels, 199

Xerox, 21

Yahoo!, 119, 137, 145

Yoga Journal, 51

Young, Louise, 218–21

Zeno's paradox, 114

Zolli, Andrew, 76

If you'd like to join the conversation on how to save the world at work, visit this book's social networking Web site: www.SavingTheWorld.net. There you'll meet other saver soldiers, learn new ways to change your business, and have fun talking about serious ideas.